Wolves, Eyes and Stormy Skies

ANTHOLOGY 4

Compiled by
Elspeth Graham and **Mal Peet**

Contents

Classic fiction
Gulliver's Travels *Jonathan Swift* 6
The Borrowers *Mary Norton* 8
The Wind in the Willows *Kenneth Grahame* 12

Classic poetry
Mushrooms *Sylvia Plath* 16
The Sea *James Reeves* 18
Cargoes *John Masefield* 19
Starling on a Green Lawn *Norman MacCaig* 20
Hen *Ted Hughes* 21

Classic drama
Peter Pan *J. M. Barrie* 22
The Tempest *William Shakespeare* 25

Biography, diary, record of observation, letters
Janet's Last Book *Allan Ahlberg* 28
Zlata's Diary *Zlata Filipovic* 30
Birds, Beasts and Relatives *Gerald Durrell* ... 33
I Realise Now That The Word I Wanted
 Was 'Naturalist' *Mal Peet* 37
A Letter from Emily 38
Part of a Letter to Emily from Mal Peet 39

Journalistic writing
Review of *Flour Babies* 40
Hen's eggs help girls learn about sex 41
Brother and sister… 42
Oh Brother! … 44
Madonna's Kid Horses Around 45

2

Non-chronological report
The Field Mushroom *Patrick Harding* 46

Established stories
Charlotte's Web *E. B. White* 48
The Wolves of Willoughby Chase *Joan Aiken* 51
The Tripods *John Christopher* 54
The Snow-Walker's Son *Catherine Fisher* 58
The December Rose *Leon Garfield* 61

Range of poetic forms
Limericks 63
Zebra (haiku) *Mal Peet* 64
Two Cinquains *Adelaide Crapsey* 65
Calligram *Guillaume Apollinaire* 66
Two Riddles *John Mole* 67
An Attempt at Unrhymed Verse *Wendy Cope* 68
My Last Nature Walk *Adrian Mitchell* 69
'You're Right,' Said Grandad *Joan Poulson* 70

Discussion texts
Should prisoners have TV sets in their cells? 72

Formal writing
A Guide to the U.N. Convention 74
Convention on the Rights of the Child 75

Work by one novelist
Flour Babies *Anne Fine* 76
Step by Wicked Step *Anne Fine* 79
Goggle Eyes *Anne Fine* 82

Work by one poet
Caterpillar *Norman MacCaig* 86
By the Canal, Early March *Norman MacCaig* 87

3

Poems on a theme
January to December *Patricia Beer* 88
It's Spring, It's Spring *Kit Wright* 90

    A Fly *Ruth Dallas* 91
    The Fly *William Blake* 92
    House Flies *N. M. Bodecker* 93
    The Fly *Ogden Nash* 93
    U.S. Flies in Hamburgers *Roger McGough* 94

Novels on a theme
Wolf *Gillian Cross* 96
White Fang *Jack London* 98
White Wolf *Henrietta Branford* 100
The Jungle Book *Rudyard Kipling* 102

A Night with a Wolf *Bayard Taylor* 104

Explanations and non-chronological reports
How do clouds stay up in the sky? *Russell Stannard* 105
Fairy Rings (mushrooms) 108
Marbles *William Bavin* 110

Style and Feature Links 112

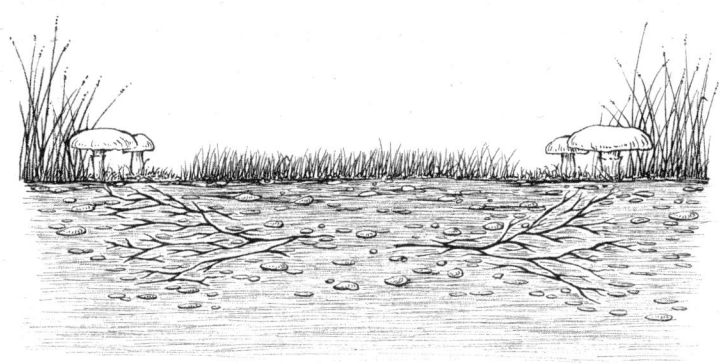

4

Introduction

Are you scared of wolves? Wolves closing in, their yellow eyes glittering in the dark? How about flies – flies in your eyes or, worse, flies in your hamburger? You may have to be brave, because there are wolves stalking through this book and flies buzzing off its pages. But maybe, just maybe, this book might change the way you feel about them.

This book is an anthology. If you look up the word in a dictionary, you will find that it means 'a collection of short pieces of writing'. The dictionary might also give you the derivation of the word – where it comes from. It comes from two Greek words: *anthos*, which means 'flower' and *logia*, which means 'collection'. The idea is that an anthology is a lovely bunch of 'word-flowers'.

You won't find many flowers in this anthology, but you will meet all those wolves and flies, plus people the size of your thumb, a joy-rider toad and a pirate with a scorched bottom. You'll find out how it feels to live in a city torn apart by war, and why a poet got a clip round the ear from his mum. If you've ever wondered why it is that clouds float, even though they're made of water, the answer is inside, and if you're reading this on a chilly autumn day, you'll be glad to know that some of the sights and sounds of spring are inside the covers of this book. (Many of these different things are connected in some way. Look at the bottom of each page for this symbol and follow the clue to the pages where you can read more ... Or you could look in the index on page 112.)

We also have two guest stars: a great poet from Scotland called Norman MacCaig, and that funny and brilliant writer Anne Fine.

We hope you find plenty to enjoy in this anthology. We hope you learn from it too. Writers learn from other writers, and if you want to be a real writer there are some great teachers in this book.

Mal Peet and Elspeth Graham

Gulliver's Travels

JONATHAN SWIFT

> Lemuel Gulliver has been shipwrecked somewhere in the South Seas. He has managed to swim to dry land where he collapses, exhausted.

I lay down on the grass, which was very short and soft, where I slept sounder than ever I remembered to have done in my life, and as I reckoned, above nine hours; for when I awaked, it was just daylight. I attempted to rise, but was not able to stir: for as I happened to lie on my back, I found my arms and legs were strongly fastened on each side to the ground; and my hair, which was long and thick, tied down in the same manner. I likewise felt several slender ligatures across my body, from my armpits to my thighs. I could only look upwards, the sun began to grow hot, and the light offended mine eyes.

I heard a confused noise about me, but in the posture I lay, could see nothing except the sky. In a little time I felt something alive moving on my left leg, which advancing gently forward over my breast, came almost up to my chin; when bending mine eyes downwards as much as I could, I perceived it to be a human creature not six inches high, with a bow and arrow in his hands, and a quiver at his back.

In the meantime, I felt at least forty more of the same kind

(as I conjectured) following the first. I was in the utmost astonishment, and roared so loud, that they all ran back in a fright; and some of them, as I was afterwards told, were hurt with the falls they got by leaping from my sides upon the ground. However, they soon returned, and one of them, who ventured so far as to get a full sight of my face, lifted up his hands and eyes by way of admiration, cried out in a shrill, but distinct voice, *Hekinah degul*: the others repeated the same words several times, but I then knew not what they meant.

I lay all this while, as the reader may believe, in great uneasiness: at length, struggling to get loose, I had the fortune to break the strings, and wrench out the pegs that fastened my left arm to the ground; for, by lifting it up to my face, I discovered the methods they had taken to bind me; and, at the same time, with a violent pull, which gave me excessive pain, I a little loosened the strings that tied down my hair on the left side, so that I was just able to turn my head about two inches.

But the creatures ran off a second time, before I could seize them; whereupon there was a great shout in a very shrill accent, and after it ceased, I heard one of them cry aloud, *Tolgo phonac*; when in an instance I felt above an hundred arrows discharged on my left hand, which pricked me like so many needles; and besides, they shot another flight into the air, as we do bombs in Europe, whereof many, I suppose, fell on my body (though I felt them not), and some on my face, which I immediately covered with my left hand.

There is more about little people on page 8.

The Borrowers

MARY NORTON

> Arrietty and her parents, Pod and Homily, are Borrowers – tiny people who lead secret lives in the houses of 'human beans'. They live by 'borrowing' from humans. Their greatest fear is being seen. In this extract, Arrietty has gone outdoors for the first time.

A greenish beetle, shining in the sunlight, came towards her across the stones. She laid her fingers lightly on its shell and it stood still, waiting and watchful, and when she moved her hand the beetle went swiftly on. An ant came hurrying in a busy zigzag. She danced in front of it to tease it and put out her foot. It stared at her, nonplussed, waving its antennae; then pettishly, as though put out, it swerved away.

Two birds came down, quarrelling shrilly, into the grass below the tree. One flew away but Arrietty could see the other among the moving grass stems above her on the slope. Cautiously she moved towards the bank and climbed a little nervously in amongst the green blades. As she parted them gently with her bare hands, drops of water plopped on her skirt and she felt the red shoes become damp. But on she went, pulling herself up now and again by rooty stems into this jungle of moss and wood-violet and creeping leaves of clover. The sharp-seeming glass blades, waist high, were tender to the touch and sprang back lightly behind her as she passed.

When at last she reached the foot of the tree, the bird took fright and flew away and she sat down suddenly on a gnarled leaf of primrose. The air was filled with scent. 'But nothing will play with you,' she thought and saw the cracks and furrows of the primrose leaves held crystal beads of dew. If she pressed the leaf these rolled like marbles.

The bank was warm, almost too warm here within the shelter of the tall grass, and the sandy earth smelled dry. Standing up, she picked a primrose. The pink stalk felt tender and living in her hands and was covered with silvery hairs, and when she held the flower, like a parasol, between her eyes and the sky, she saw the sun's pale light through the veined petals.

On a piece of bark she found a wood-louse and she struck it lightly with her swaying flower. It curled immediately and became a ball, bumping softly away downhill amongst the grass roots. But she knew about wood-lice. There were plenty of them at home under the floor. Homily always scolded her if she played with them because, she said, they smelled of old knives.

She lay back among the stalks of the primroses and they

made a coolness between her and the sun, and then, sighing, she turned her head and looked sideways up the bank among the grass stems. Startled, she caught her breath. Something had moved above her on the bank. Something had glittered. Arrietty stared.

Chapter Nine

It was an eye. Or it looked like an eye. Clear and bright like the colour of the sky. An eye like her own but enormous. A glaring eye. Breathless with fear, she sat up. And the eye blinked. A great fringe of lashes came curving down and flew up again out of sight. Cautiously, Arrietty moved her legs: she would slide noiselessly in among the grass stems and slither away down the bank.

'Don't move!' said a voice, and the voice, like the eye, was enormous but, somehow, hushed – and hoarse like a surge of wind through the grating on a stormy night in March.

Arrietty froze. 'So this is it,' she thought, 'the worst and most terrible thing of all: I have been "seen"! Whatever happened to Eggletina will now, almost certainly happen to me!'

There was a pause and Arrietty, her heart pounding in her ears, heard the breath again drawn swiftly into the vast lungs. 'Or,' said the voice, whispering still, 'I shall hit you with my ash stick.'

Suddenly Arrietty became calm. 'Why?' she asked. How strange her own voice sounded! Crystal thin and harebell clear, it tinkled on the air.

'In case,' came the surprised whisper at last, 'you ran towards me, quickly, through the grass… in case,' it went on, trembling a little, 'you scrabbled at me with your nasty little hands.'

Arrietty stared at the eye; she held herself quite still. 'Why?' she asked again, and again the word tinkled – icy cold it sounded this time, and needle sharp.

'Things do,' said the voice. 'I've seen them. In India.'

Arrietty thought of her Gazetteer of the World. 'You're not in India now,' she pointed out.

There is more about little people on page 6.

The Wind in the Willows

Kenneth Grahame

> Mr Toad is mad about cars and a crazy driver. Here, he has been found guilty of stealing, dangerous driving and, worst of all, being cheeky to the police.

'To my mind,' observed the Chairman of the Bench of Magistrates cheerfully, 'the *only* difficulty that presents itself in this otherwise very clear case is, how we can possibly make it sufficiently hot for the incorrigible rogue and hardened ruffian whom we see cowering in the dock before us. Let me see: he has been found guilty, on the clearest evidence, first, of stealing a valuable motor-car; secondly, of driving to the public danger; and, thirdly, of gross impertinence to the rural police. Mr Clerk, will you tell us, please, what is the very stiffest penalty we can impose for each of these offences? Without, of course, giving the prisoner the benefit of any doubt, because there isn't any.'

The clerk scratched his nose with his pen. 'Some people would consider,' he observed, 'that stealing the motor-car was the worst offence; and so it is. But cheeking the police undoubtedly carries the severest penalty; and so it ought. Supposing you were to say twelve months for the theft, which is mild; and three years for the furious driving, which is lenient; and fifteen years for the cheek, which was pretty bad sort of cheek, judging by what we've heard from the witness-box, even if you only believe one-tenth part of what you heard, and I never believe more myself – those figures, if added together correctly, tot up to nineteen years –'

'First rate!' said the Chairman.

'– So you had better make it a round twenty years and be on the safe side,' concluded the Clerk.

'An excellent suggestion!' said the Chairman approvingly. 'Prisoner! Pull yourself together and try and stand up straight. It's going to be twenty years for you this time. And mind, if you appear before us again, upon any charge whatever, we shall have to deal with you very seriously!'

Then the brutal minions of the law fell upon the hapless Toad; loaded him with chains, and dragged him from the Court House, shrieking, praying, protesting; across the market-place, where the playful populace, always as severe upon detected crime as they were sympathetic and helpful when one is merely 'wanted', assailed him with jeers, carrots, and popular catchwords; past hooting school children, their innocent faces lit up with the pleasure they ever derive from the sight of a gentleman in difficulties; across the hollow-sounding drawbridge, below the spiky portcullis, under the frowning archway of the grim old castle, whose ancient towers soared high overhead; past guardrooms full of grinning soldiery off duty, past sentries who coughed in a horrid sarcastic way, because that is as much as a sentry on his post dare do to show his contempt and abhorrence of crime; up time-worn winding stairs, past men-at-arms in casquet and corselet of steel, darting threatening looks through their vizards; across the courtyards, where mastiffs strained at their leash and pawed the air to get at him; past ancient warders, their halberds leant against the wall, dozing over a pasty and a flagon of brown ale; on and on, past the rack-chamber and the thumbscrewroom, past the turning that led to the private scaffold, till they reached the door of the grimmest dungeon that lay in the heart of the innermost keep. There at last they paused, where an ancient gaoler sat fingering a bunch of mighty keys.

Mushrooms

SYLVIA PLATH

Overnight, very
Whitely, discreetly,
Very quietly
Our toes, our noses
Take hold on the loam,
Acquire the air.

Nobody sees us,
Stops us, betrays us;
The small grains make room.

Soft fists insist on
Heaving the needles,
The leafy bedding,

Even the paving.
Our hammers, our rams,
Earless and eyeless,

Perfectly voiceless,
Widen the crannies,
Shoulder through holes. We

Diet on water,
On crumbs of shadow,
Bland-mannered, asking

Little or nothing.
So many of us!
So many of us!

We are shelves, we are
Tables, we are meek,
We are edible,

Nudgers and shovers
In spite of ourselves,
Our kind multiplies;

We shall by morning
Inherit the earth.
Our foot's in the door.

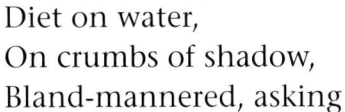

The Sea

JAMES REEVES

The sea is a hungry dog,
Giant and grey.
He rolls on the beach all day.
With his clashing teeth and shaggy jaws
Hour upon hour he gnaws
The rumbling, tumbling stones,
And 'Bones, bones, bones, bones!'
The giant sea-dog moans,
Licking his greasy paws.

And when the night wind roars
And the moon rocks in the stormy cloud,
He bounds to his feet and snuffs and sniffs,
Shaking his wet sides over the cliffs,
And howls and hollos long and loud.

But on quiet days in May or June,
When even the grasses on the dune
Play no more their reedy tune,
With his head between his paws
He lies on the sandy shores,
So quiet, so quiet, he scarcely snores.

Cargoes

JOHN MASEFIELD

Quinquereme of Nineveh from distant Ophir
Rowing home to haven in sunny Palestine,
With a cargo of ivory,
And apes and peacocks,
Sandalwood, cedarwood, and sweet white wine.

Stately Spanish galleon coming from the Isthmus,
Dipping through the Tropics by the palm-green shores,
With a cargo of diamonds,
Emeralds, amethysts,
Topazes, and cinnamon, and gold moidores.

Dirty British coaster with a salt-caked smoke stack
Butting through the Channel in the mad March days,
With a cargo of Tyne coal,
Road-rail, pig-lead,
Firewood, iron-ware, and cheap tin trays.

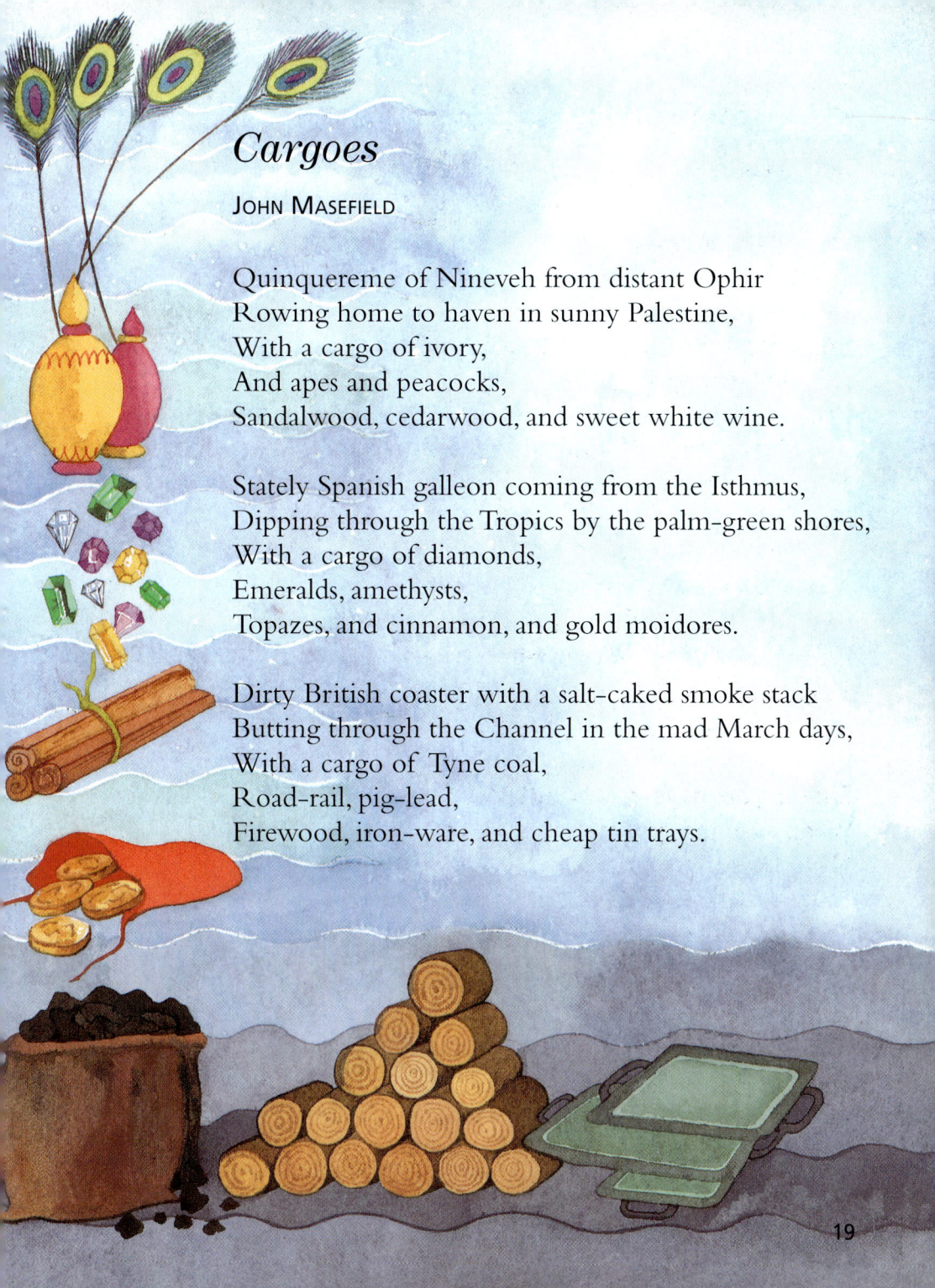

Starling on a Green Lawn

NORMAN MACCAIG

He makes such a business of going somewhere
he's like a hopping with a bird in it.

The somewhere's an any place, which he recognises at once.
His track is zig–zag   zig   zag–zag.

He angles himself to the sun and his blackness
becomes something fallen from a stained-glass window.

He's a guy King, a guy Prince, though his only royal habit
is to walk with his hands clasped behind his back.

Now he's flown up like a mad glove on to a fence post.
He squinnies at the world and draws a cork from a bottle.

There is more about birds on page 21.
Other poems by Norman MacCaig are on pages 86 and 87.

Hen

TED HUGHES

Dowdy the Hen
Has nothing to do
But peer and peck, and peck and peer
At nothing.

Sometimes a couple of scratches to right
Sometimes a couple of scratches to left
And sometimes head-up, red-rimmed stare
At nothing.

A Hen in your pen, O Hen, O when
Will something happen?
Nothing to do but brood on her nest
And wish.

Wish? Wish? What shall she wish for?
Stealthy fingers
Under her bum.
An egg on your dish.

 There is more about birds on page 20.

Peter Pan

J. M. Barrie

> We're in Never Land. Wicked Captain Hook is leading his pirate crew in the hunt for his arch-enemy Peter Pan, leader of the Lost Boys.

HOOK Scatter and look for them. *(The boatswain whistles his instructions, and the men disperse on their frightful errand. With none to hear save* SMEE, HOOK *becomes confidential.)* Most of all I want their captain, Peter Pan. 'Twas he cut off my arm. I have waited long to shake his hand with this. *(Luxuriating)* Oh, I'll tear him!

SMEE *(always ready for a chat)*. Yet I have oft heard you say your hook was worth a score of hands, for combing the hair and other homely uses.

HOOK If I was a mother I would pray to have my children born with this instead of that *(his left arm creeps nervously behind him. He has a galling remembrance)*. Smee, Pan flung my arm to a crocodile that happened to be passing by.

SMEE I have often noticed your strange dread of crocodiles.

HOOK *(pettishly)*. Not of crocodiles but of that one crocodile. *(He lays bare a lacerated heart.)* The brute liked my arm so much, Smee, that he has followed me ever since, from sea to sea, and from land to land, licking his lips for the rest of me.

SMEE *(looking for the bright side)*. In a way it is a sort of compliment.

HOOK *(with dignity)*. I want no such compliments; I want Peter Pan, who first gave the brute his taste for me. Smee, that crocodile would have had me before now, but by a lucky chance he swallowed a clock, and it goes tick, tick, tick, tick inside him; and so before he can reach me I hear the tick and

bolt. *(He emits a hollow rumble.)* Once I heard it strike six within him.

SMEE *(sombrely)*. Some day the clock will run down, and then he'll get you.

HOOK *(a broken man)*. Ay, that is the fear that haunts me. *(He rises.)* Smee, this seat is hot; odds, bobs, hammer and tongs, I am burning.

(He has been sitting, he thinks, on one of the island mushrooms, which are of enormous size. But this is a hand-painted one placed here in times of danger to conceal a chimney. They remove it, and tell-tale smoke issues; also, alas, the sound of children's voices.)

SMEE A chimney!

HOOK *(avidly)* Listen! Smee, 'tis plain they live here, beneath the ground. *(He replaces the mushroom. His brain works tortuously.)*

SMEE *(hopefully).* Unrip your plan, Captain.

HOOK To return to the boat and cook a large rich cake of jolly thickness with sugar on it, green sugar. There can be but one room below, for there is but one chimney. The silly moles had not the sense to see that they did not need a door apiece. We must leave the cake on the shore of the mermaids' lagoon. These boys are always swimming about there, trying to catch the mermaids. They will find the cake and gobble it up, because, having no mother, they don't know how dangerous 'tis to eat rich damp cake. They will die!

SMEE *(fascinated).* It is the wickedest, prettiest policy I ever heard of.

The Tempest

WILLIAM SHAKESPEARE

> Stephano and Trinculo have been shipwrecked and cast up on an island where they find a half-human monster called Caliban. Caliban has decided that Stephano will be his new master. The three of them are plotting to murder Prospero, the ruler of the island. But Prospero is a magician, and his 'airy Spirit', Ariel, finds out what's going on.

Enter Ariel, invisible.

Caliban: As I told thee before, I am subject to a tyrant –
A sorcerer, that by his cunning hath
Cheated me of the island.
Ariel: Thou liest.
Caliban *(turning on Trinculo):* Thou liest, thou jesting monkey, thou!
I would my valiant master would destroy thee…
I do not lie.
Stephano: Trinculo, if thou trouble him any more in's tale, by this hand, I will supplant some of your teeth.
Trinculo: Why, I said nothing.
Stephano: Mum, then, and no more. *(to Caliban):* Proceed.
Caliban: I say, by sorcery he got this isle –
From me he has got it. If thy greatness will
Revenge it on him – for I know thou darest,
But this thing *(pointing to Trinculo)* dare not –
Stephano: That's most certain.
Caliban: Thou shalt be lord of it, and I will serve thee.
Stephano: How now shall this be compassed? Canst thou bring me to the party?
Caliban: Yea, yea, my lord, I'll yield him thee asleep,
Where thou mayest knock a nail into his head.

Ariel: Thou liest, thou canst not.
Caliban: What a pied ninny's this! Thou scurvy patch!
I do beseech thy greatness, give him blows,
And take his bottle from him: when that's gone,
He shall drink nought but brine, for I'll not
show him where the quick freshes are.
Stephano: Trinculo, run into no further danger: interrupt
the monster one word further, and by this hand,
I'll turn my mercy out of doors, and make a
stock-fish of thee.
Trinculo: Why? What did I? I did nothing: I'll go further
off.
Stephano: Didst thou not say he lied?
Ariel: Thou liest.
Stephano: Do I so? Take thou that! *(beats Trinculo)*.

Eventually, Caliban, Stephano and Trinculo set off to find Prospero. Ariel, who is still invisible, plays a loud tune on a pipe and drum, which scares Stephano and Trinculo out of their wits.

Caliban: Be not afeard – the isle is full of noises,
Sounds and sweet airs, that give delight and hurt not:
Sometimes a thousand twangling instruments
Will hum about mine ears; and sometimes voices,
That, if I had then waked after long sleep,
Will make me sleep again – and then, in dreaming,
The clouds methought would open, and show riches
Ready to drop upon me, that when I waked
I cried to dream again.

Janet's Last Book

ALLAN AHLBERG

The scarf

It is September, nine o'clock one morning. I have taken up her breakfast tray: porridge, maple syrup, glass of milk, plus a few other things: Tylex and Voltarol for the pain, Zantac to protect her stomach lining from some of the other drugs, Maxolon and Kytril for sickness after chemotherapy.

The sun comes in at the window. I pull up a chair and sit beside the bed. Janet sips her milk through a straw. She looks at me, mildly – her usual gaze, then past me, over my shoulder to something on the mantelpiece.

'Rose'd like that scarf,' she says.

◆

Some people, as their lives go by, acknowledge death, talk of it, let it out and look at it from time to time. Others, the majority perhaps, don't, preferring to stay mum. Jan was one of these. She had been gripped by breast cancer for almost two years. It had spread to her bones and now her liver. Well, she had read the books and BACUP pamphlets, was realistic and knew the score. She had her massive fears and tiny hopes (until the very end), but said nothing. Until this day.

'Rose'd like that scarf,' she said.

I knew entirely what she meant. It was her first bequest.

◆

So Jan began to deal with death. Typically, for her, she approached it first with presents. She had a small notebook, a page per person. Often the items were drawn as well as listed. There was, however, no particular system. The whole thing was simply driven by her powerful memory. She just recalled that someone once had expressed a liking for something: '*Byron:* Fish poster in studio', or was present when something else was bought: '*Felicity:* Turquoise shoes with heels and bow'.

Janet dealt with death, faced it, hated it.

She didn't want to leave; the party was still going on. There was a manuscript waiting, proofs in the pipeline, a plaintive cat stationed by the fridge and Red Dwarf on the telly. Most of all, of course, there was Jessica (nearly fifteen), her beloved daughter.

The days passed. Janet's life was shrunk to a little patch, a few hours in the afternoon downstairs on the chesterfield. A couple of times she spoke of her own funeral. Jan was not religious. She wanted a secular ceremony and burial in the local cemetery. It was her wish that family and friends would gather together, sing a bit and speak for her. She wasn't solemn either. At one point, smiling her slight sly smile, she said, 'Tell Graham he's allowed to say "bum" ' (guaranteed with her to get a laugh).

It's February now. Janet has been dead three months. In the bedroom her last-worn clothes hang over the end of the bed, her numerous shoes still clutter the floor and her perfume lingers (mainly because I spray it around from time to time). On the mantelpiece: some talc, some rings, a foolish-looking knitted rabbit and a polystyrene head with a wig on it, bought just in case and luckily (!) not needed. There is a box of bargain jewels … but no scarf.

Zlata's Diary: A Child's Life in Sarajevo

Zlata Filipovic

Wednesday, 27 May 1992

Dear Mimmy,
SLAUGHTER! MASSACRE! HORROR! CRIME! BLOOD! SCREAMS! TEARS! DESPAIR!

That's what Vaso Miskin Street looks like today. Two shells exploded in the street and one in the market. Mummy was near by at the time. She ran to Grandma's and Grandad's. Daddy and I were beside ourselves because she hadn't come home. I saw some of it on TV but I still can't believe what I actually saw. It's unbelievable. I've got a lump in my throat and a knot in my tummy. HORRIBLE. They're taking the wounded to the hospital. It's a madhouse. We kept going to the window hoping to see Mummy, but she wasn't back. They released a list of the dead and wounded. Daddy and I were tearing our hair out. We didn't know what had happened to her. Was she alive? At 16.00 Daddy decided to go and check the hospital. He got dressed, and I got ready to go to the Bobars', so as not to stay at home alone. I looked out the window one more time and ... I SAW MUMMY RUNNING ACROSS THE BRIDGE. As she came into the house she started shaking and crying. Through her tears she told us how she had seen dismembered bodies. All the neighbours came because they had been afraid for her. Thank God, Mummy is with us. Thank God.

A HORRIBLE DAY. UNFORGETTABLE. HORRIBLE! HORRIBLE!

Thursday, 2 July 1992

Dear Mimmy,
We gave ourselves a treat today. We picked the cherries off the tree in the yard and ate them all up. We had watched it blossom and its small green fruits slowly turn red and now here we were eating them. Oh, you're a wonderful cherry tree! The plum tree hasn't got any fruit so we won't even get to try it! I miss fruit a lot. In these days of war in Sarajevo, there is no basic food or any of the other things a person needs, and there is no fruit. But now I can say that I ate myself silly on cherries.

    Braco, Mummy's brother, is getting better. He's even walking a bit now.
    Zlata

Monday, 15 March 1993

Dear Mimmy,
I'm sick again. My throat hurts, I'm sneezing and coughing. And spring is around the corner. The second spring of the war. I know from the calendar, but I don't see it. I can't see it because I can't feel it. All I can see are the poor people still lugging water, and the even poorer casualties – young people without arms and legs. They're the ones who had the fortune or perhaps the misfortune to survive.

There are no trees to blossom and no birds, because the war has destroyed them as well. There is no sound of birds twittering in springtime. There aren't even any pigeons – the symbol of Sarajevo. No noisy children, no games. Even the children no longer seem like children. They've had their childhood taken away from them, and without that they can't be children. It's as if Sarajevo is slowly dying, disappearing. Life is disappearing. So how can I feel spring, when spring is something that awakens life, and here there is no life, here everything seems to have died.

I'm sad again, Mimmy. But you have to know that I'm getting sadder and sadder. I'm sad wherever I think, and I have to think.
Your Zlata

Birds, Beasts and Relatives

GERALD DURRELL

It was in this bay that I caught my first spider crab. I would have walked right past him thinking him to be a weed-covered rock, if he had not made an incautious movement. His body was about the size and shape of a small flattened pear and at the pointed end it was decorated with a series of spikes, ending in two horn-like protuberances over his eyes. His legs and his pincers were long, slender and spindly. But the thing that intrigued me most was the fact that he was wearing, on his back and on his legs, a complete suit of tiny sea-weeds, which appeared to be growing out of his shell.

Enchanted by this weird creature, I carried him triumphantly along the beach to my rock pool and placed him in it. The firm grip with which I had had to hold him (for once having discovered that he was recognized as a crab he made desperate efforts to escape) had rubbed off quite a lot of his sea-weed suit by the time I got him to the pool. I placed him in the shallow, clear water and, lying on my stomach, watched him to see what he would do. Standing high on his toes, like a spider in a hurry, he scuttled a foot or so away from where I had put him and then froze.

He sat like this for a long time, so long in fact that I was just deciding that he was going to remain immobile for the rest of the morning, recovering from the shock of capture, when he suddenly extended a long, delicate claw and very daintily, almost shyly, plucked a tiny piece of sea-weed which was growing on a nearby rock. He put the sea-weed to his mouth and I could see him mumbling at it.

At first I thought he was eating it, but I soon realized I was mistaken for, with angular grace, he placed his claw over his back, felt around in a rather fumbling sort of way, and then

33

planted the tiny piece of weed on his carapace. I presumed that he had been making the base of the weed sticky with saliva or some similar substance to make it adhere to his back.

As I watched him, he trundled slowly round the pool collecting a variety of sea-weed with the assiduous dedication of a professional botanist in a hitherto unexplored jungle. Within an hour or so his back was covered with such a thick layer of growth that, if he sat still and I took my eyes off him for a moment, I had difficulty in knowing exactly where he was.

Intrigued by this cunning form of camouflage, I searched the bay carefully until I found another spider crab. For him I built a special pool with a sandy floor, completely devoid of weed. I put him in and he settled down quite happily. The following day I returned, carrying me a nail brush (which turned out to be Larry's) and, taking the unfortunate spider crab, scrubbed him vigorously until not an atom of weed remained on his back or

legs. Then I dropped into his pool a variety of things; a number of tiny top shells and some broken fragments of coral, some small sea anemones and some minute bits of bottle glass which had been sandpapered by the sea so that they looked like misty jewels. Then I sat down to watch.

The crab, when returned to his pool, sat quite still for several minutes, obviously recovering from the indignity of the scrubbing I had given him. Then, as if he could not quite believe the terrible fate that had overtaken him, he put his two pincers over his head and felt his back with the utmost delicacy, presumably hoping against hope that at least one frond of sea-weed remained. But I had done my task well and his back was shining and bare.

He walked a few paces tentatively and then squatted down and sulked for half an hour. Then he roused himself out of his gloom, walked over to the edge of the pond and tried to wedge himself under a dark ridge of rock. There he sat brooding miserably over his lack of camouflage until it was time for me to go home.

I returned very early the following morning and, to my delight, saw that the crab had been busy while I had been away. Making the best of a bad job, he had decorated the top of his shell with a number of the ingredients that I had left for him. He looked extremely gaudy and had an air of carnival about him. Striped top shells had been pasted on, interspersed with bits of coral and up near his head he was wearing two beadlet anemones, like an extremely saucy bonnet with ribbons. I thought, as I watched him crawling about the sand, that he looked exceedingly conspicuous, but, curiously enough, when he went over and squatted by his favourite overhang of rock, he turned into what appeared to be a little pile of shell and coral debris, with a couple of anemones perched on top of it.

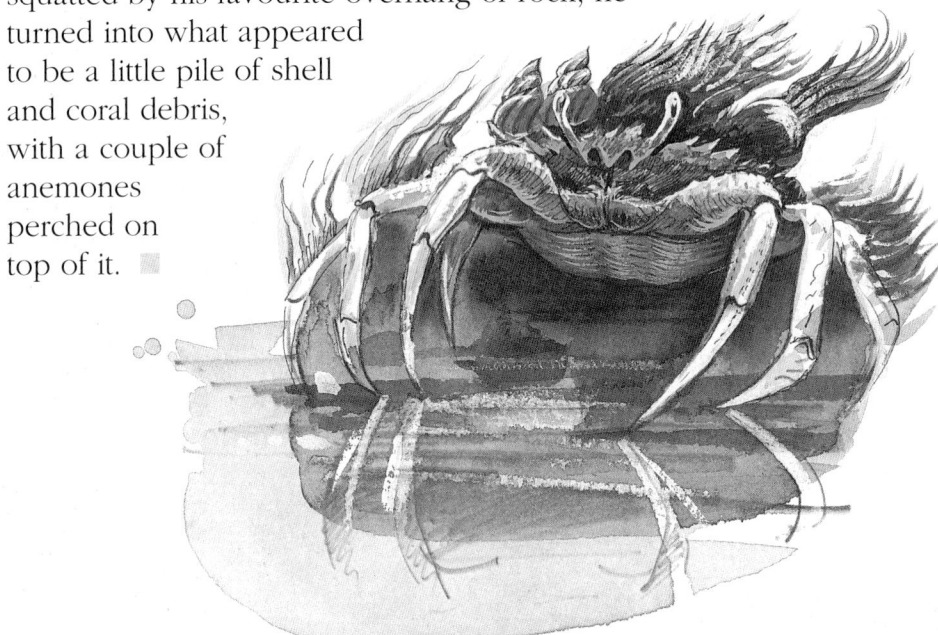

There is more about naturalists and autobiography on pages 37, 38 and 39.

I Realise Now That The Word I Wanted Was 'Naturalist'

MAL PEET

I love the Natural History Museum. There's so much stuff in it.
Fossils and dinosaurs and weird, weird things.
I can't get enough of it.
The first time you go there,
you walk past things that seem to be boring,
like glass cases and diagrams and books full of drawing.
Then the next time you go, you stop and look.
And that's it. You're hooked.

I was very young when this happened to me.
One day I came home from
the Natural History Museum
and said to my mum,
"I'm going to be a naturist."
She was hanging washing on
   the line,
but she gave me a clip round
   the ear anyway
and said, "No son of mine
is going to go around
   with no clothes on."

There is more about naturalists and autobiography on pages 33, 38 and 39.

A letter from Emily

Mount Pleasant Primary School

November 5, 1998

Mal Peet
C/o Collins Educational
77-85 Fulham Palace Road
Hammersmith
London W6 8JB

Dear Mal Peet,

In our class we are doing some work about autobiography. Mrs Samuels says that all sorts of writing can be autobiographical, they don't have to be just the story of your own life.

I read your poem called 'I Realise Now That The Word I Wanted Was "Naturalist" '. I didn't understand it the first time but then Mrs Samuels got me to look the words up in the dictionary and then it made me laugh.

The poem is written in the first person (I). So is it autobiographical? Is it a true story? Did you grow up to be a naturalist or do you just write poems?

Mrs Samuels said it was OK to write to you but she said that writers are sometimes too busy to answer and I should not be disappointed if you don't reply, so it's OK if you don't.

I've never been to the Natural History Museum. Where is it? Does it have huge skeletons in it, like the one in the picture?

I think the poem is really good.

Sincerely,

Emily O'Donnell

Emily O'Donnell
Aged $10\frac{1}{2}$

There is more about naturalists and autobiography on pages 33, 37 and 39.

Part of a Letter to Emily from Mal Peet

The poem called 'I Realise Now That The Word I Wanted Was "Naturalist"' is autobiographical, but that doesn't mean that it's completely true. For instance, the Natural History Museum is in London, and I grew up a long way from there. I was an adult when I first visited it (and fell in love with it).

What is true is that when I was a small boy I was fascinated by animals. So I decided that when I grew up I'd be… well, I thought the word was 'naturist'. People who study science are called scientists, so someone who studies nature would be a naturist, right? Wrong, as it turned out. When I told my mother that I was going to be a naturist, I got a very strange reaction. This brings me to the second lie in the poem. My mum didn't clip me round the ear. She just said 'Don't be so daft.' 'What's daft about it?' I wanted to know. 'You're just being dirty-minded like all little boys,' she said. This was very confusing.

I had a teacher at Primary School called Mr Pinkerton. I plucked up the courage to tell him about my wanting to be a naturist and about my mum's strange reaction to the idea. Mr Pinkerton went pink. He actually *giggled*. I was a bit shocked.

'Do you know what a naturist is?' he asked, smiling. So I started to talk about dinosaurs, chameleons, bees… and then he held his hand up to stop me. "I think you've made a small mistake,' he said kindly. 'A naturist is someone who, er, prefers not to wear clothes. Who likes to spend time in the… er… nude.'

I went even pinker than Mr Pinkerton.

'*Naturists* is the proper name for people we usually call "nudists", Mr Pinkerton said. 'I think the word you want is *naturalist*.'

When I was writing poems about animals this memory came back to me, and I put it together with my love of the Natural History Museum. So yes, the poem is autobiographical. You could even say that it's true, in a sense, even though it's not quite factual.

There is more about naturalists and autobiography on pages 36, 37 and 38.

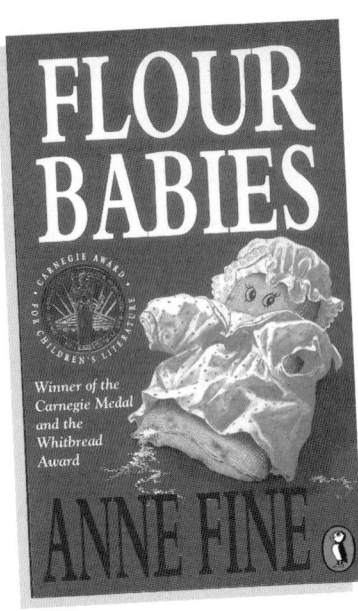

Review of *Flour Babies*

Flour Babies
Anne Fine, Puffin
0 14 036147 2   £3.50

A superb book: Anne Fine makes wonderful stories out of the unlikeliest of material, blending comedy with a fine streak of poignant human understanding. All the pupils do a science project, but these pupils are the lowest of the low and take on sacks of flour as babies to which they act as surrogate fathers. It begins with a misunderstanding as Simon Martin is sure he overhears the promise of being able to explode the flour sacks at the end but, for Simon, the flour sack becomes a real baby to which he talks earnestly, trying to solve the question of his own father leaving him as an infant. The interrogation is both moving and very funny and the finale – well! After *Madam Doubtfire* let's hope they film this.
A.J.

Flour Babies shines out like a beacon. A beautifully crafted book, very funny, and often moving, yet completely unsentimental. Sarah O'Reilly, *Time Out*

Books For Keeps No. 88 September 1994

(Note: *Flour Babies* won the Carnegie Medal and the Whitbread Award for best children's novel.)

There is more about *Flour Babies* on page 76.

Hen's eggs help girls learn about sex

A HEN'S EGG is the latest recruit in the battle to stop unwanted pregnancies. Teenage girls are being encouraged to care for an egg as if it were a baby, to give them a taste of life as carer and guardian.

Dozens of schools in London are taking part in the initiative, organised by local health authorities and the Brook Advisory Centres.

Each girl is encouraged to look after an egg for a week as if it were her own baby. She prepares a carrycot, lined with tissues, which she keeps with her at all times. The girl feeds and changes the egg six times a day, by replacing the tissues, and keeps a diary of the egg's progress.

Instructions issued to pupils aged 14 and 15 at the Maria Fidelis Convent School in Camden stress that the egg must go everywhere with the girls during the exercise.

"If you go out, you may put your egg in your carrycot in your bag but remember never to leave your bag unattended and don't swing your bag about as you may break the egg.

Louise Jury
The Guardian

"If you break your egg you must tell someone at home and pay a pre-arranged fine (perhaps the price of an egg) or do a household chore. Record it in your diary, stating how you broke it, how you felt about it and the reactions of the person you told. Get a new egg and continue with the exercise."

A Camden council spokeswoman said it was part of a sex education project that was often followed up by encouraging the teenagers to look after dolls simulating babies.

"We all know about the huge problem of unwanted teenage pregnancies. This is an imaginative project designed to get teenagers to really think about the consequences of unwanted pregnancies."

There is more about learning to care for babies on pages 40 and 76.

Brother and sister meet again after 80 years apart

Simon Cooper
The *Guardian*

A BROTHER and sister who were separated after being orphaned in England during the First World War have been reunited in Canada more than 80 years later.

Daisy Bance, 85, from Southampton, and her brother Albert, 84, were put in different children's homes after their father was killed in the trenches. They never saw each other again.

When Mr Bance was 14, he was shipped to Canada to start a new life as one of the so-called Home Children, while Miss Bance remained in Britain.

But on Monday, the pair met again during a reunion at Montreal airport.

Hugging her brother, Miss Bance said: "I don't want to let you go anymore."

Mr Bance replied: "Here I am, I'm your brother. I've been waiting a lifetime."

Last night Miss Bance added: "It's wonderful. It's

Albert Bance embraces his sister Daisy in Montreal 80 years after they were parted as war orphans

come from nowhere. I had given up hope of finding Albert again."

She described the moment their years of separation ended: "There were all these people standing there and there was Albert with a lovely bouquet of flowers. I just put my arms around him and started crying."

The reunion was arranged by Mr Bance's children and grandchildren, who spent several years trying to trace his sister.

After finding her birth certificate in the Family Records Office in London, they began tracing all the Bances in the south of England. They searched the Internet, and sent letters to possible relatives until she was found.

The brother and sister swapped faxes and in October enjoyed their first telephone call. They met after one of Mr Bance's five children won a radio competition in Canada to bring a family together for Christmas.

The reunion trip is Miss Bance's first trip abroad. She says she made the 3,000 mile journey because "I thought it would be a disappointment to Albert if I did not come."

After the siblings' father was killed in France in the dying months of the war, their mother took them from their home in Putney, south west London, and placed Albert, Daisy and another sister, Frances, in children's homes. She is thought to have died shortly afterwards.

Miss Bance, who has never married, lived in nine orphans' homes throughout England before entering service as a live-in help to a series of wealthy families. She retired to Southampton where she now lives.

After arriving in Canada in 1929, Mr Bance worked on a farm in the Eastern Townships. He later married, joined the police force and then served as a fire chief before retiring. His wife, Evelyn, died three years ago and he now lives in Waterloo, Quebec.

Mr Bance's daughter, Joan Alexander, said her father would spend the week getting to know his sister. The family is planning a dinner for tomorrow.

Mrs Alexander said: "It's the most wonderful thing. It's almost overwhelming.

"My father was so nervous because he was only four when they were separated. The family had been collecting information about the two sisters for years. We think Frances has died, but we were delighted when we finally managed to contact Daisy."

OH BROTHER!
DAISY AND ALBERT TOGETHER AGAIN AFTER A LIFETIME APART

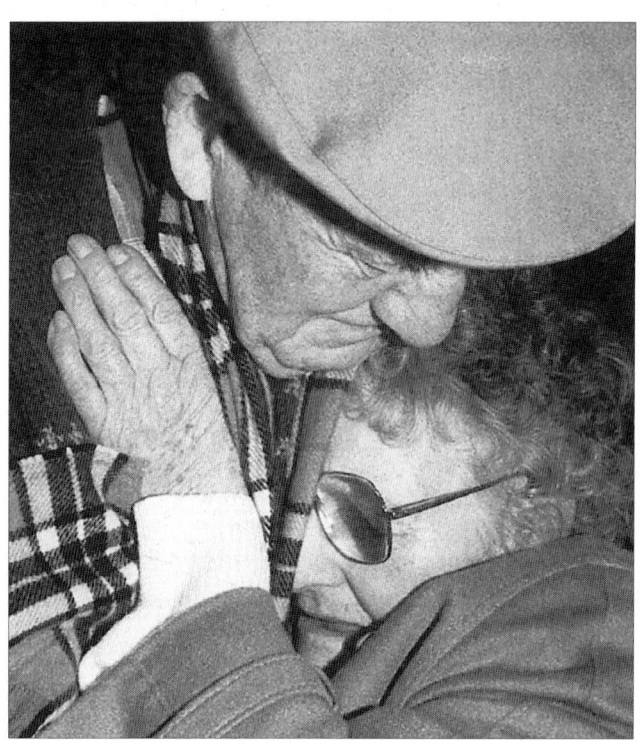

The hug that waited 80 years

Daisy Bance flew into Montreal yesterday – and straight into the arms of the brother she last saw in 1918.

Daisy, 85, and her brother Albert Bance, 84, were **torn apart** after their war-hero father died just weeks before the end of World War I. Their mother put them into different children's homes, and they never saw each other again. Until yesterday. When Albert was 14 he was **shipped out** to Canada, and began a new life as a farm boy. Daisy lived in **nine** different orphanages before becoming a servant in a number of posh houses all over England.

Prize

Albert's children and grandchildren spent years trying to trace his sister. In the end, they found her through the **internet**. She had retired and was living in Southampton. The couple swopped faxes in October; but it was only after one of Albertís children won a radio competition prize that they could end the 80-year separation and bring long-lost brother and sister together for Christmas.

Tears

And at Montreal airport yesterday, tears washed the years away. Daisy wrapped her arms around her brother and sobbed 'I don't want to let you go any more.' Albert, a big strong man, fought to control his emotion. 'I'm here,' he whispered, 'I'm your brother. I've waited a lifetime.'

The American Globe

MADONNA'S KID HORSES AROUND!

Little Lourdes is the cutest cowgirl in town

Ride'em wow-girl! Madonna's adorable tot Lourdes – Lola to her pals – is only 2½, but she already loves to play the ponies!

The cute little cowgirl had a blast when a nanny and body-guard brought her to the $1.50 pony rides at Los Angeles' Griffith Park, even though neither her mom Madonna nor her father, fitness instructor Carlos Leon, 32, were anywhere in sight.

> *'It was a great opportunity for her to play like a normal kid'*

'I'm sure Madonna would have loved to have been there with her,' an eyewitness reports to the GLOBE, 'but because she wasn't, few people noticed Lourdes and it was a great opportunity for the youngster to play like a normal kid.'

Although Madonna, 40, used to be known as the queen of do-your-own-thing, since becoming a mother she has been raising her daughter with strict old-fashioned values – and it shows.

'Lourdes doesn't seem spoiled at all,' says the eyewitness. 'She's very polite. She always says please and thank you and she wasn't the least bit demanding of her nanny or the other kids. She's as cute as a button.'

The Field Mushroom

FROM *HOW TO IDENTIFY EDIBLE MUSHROOMS* BY PATRICK HARDING

The most well-known wild species and for many people the only one deemed safe to eat; all others being considered dangerous toadstools. 'Mushrooms are edible and I know a mushroom when I see one' is a common boast, but the fact is that not all the 40-odd British mushroom species are edible, and the problem is knowing which mushroom has been collected. The Yellow-staining Mushroom is easily mistaken for the Field Mushroom and may produce alarming symptoms: for every wild fungus, accurate identification is essential.

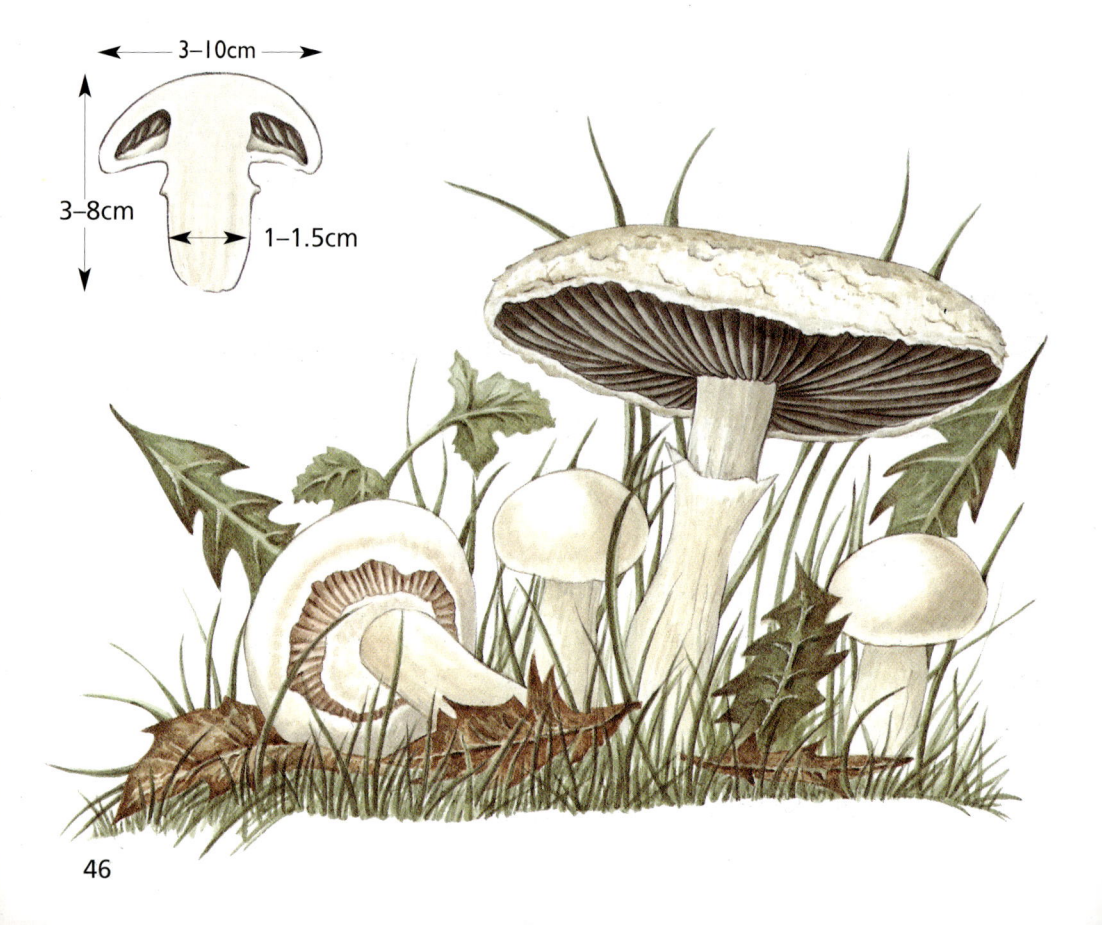

KEY FEATURES Young specimens have crowded, bright pink gills enclosed in a white veil. At maturity the gills are free and dark chocolate brown (the spore colour), the cut white flesh colours faintly pink.

HABITAT Grass kept short by grazing or mowing including meadows, parks, lawns, golf courses and woodland rides.

FREQUENCY Common. Locally abundant, sometimes in fairy rings.

SEASON Early summer to late autumn, especially after rain (see histogram).

CAP The button stage is white, dry, firm and domed. The margins are covered with remnants of the veil and remain inrolled until maturity when the centre of the now flat cap may break up into small, pale brown scales.

GILLS At first totally enclosed in a white veil. Crowded and free. Ageing from deep pink through chocolate brown to black when they become soft and wet.

SPORE PRINT Very dark brown (see picture).

STEM Short, white, bruises brown. Solid then spongy. Simple, white, thin, transient ring.

FLESH Soft and white, with slight reddening in cut stem. Smell and taste stronger than most shop mushrooms.

Fruiting season

Month	
J	
F	
M	
A	
M	
J	🍄🍄🍄🍄
J	🍄
A	🍄🍄
S	🍄🍄🍄🍄🍄🍄🍄🍄🍄
O	🍄🍄🍄🍄🍄🍄
N	🍄🍄🍄
D	

Cooking and Eating

The most versatile of all edible fungi and small ones can safely be eaten raw (sliced in salads). 'Flats' can be stuffed (include the chopped stem) and baked. They do not have to be peeled. Old specimens are prone to maggots especially in the stem.

There is more about mushrooms on pages 16 and 108.

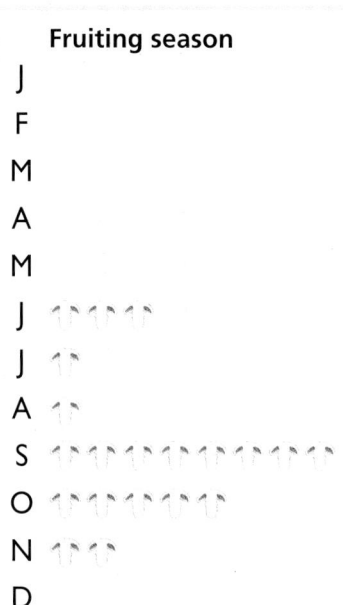

Charlotte's Web

E. B. White

> On Zuckerman's farm, Charlotte the spider has a plan to save the life of her best friend, Wilbur the pig. By weaving messages praising Wilbur she hopes to persuade the humans that Wilbur is too special to be eaten.

A Meeting

One evening, a few days after the writing had appeared in Charlotte's web, the spider called a meeting of all the animals in the barn cellar.

'I shall begin by calling the roll. Wilbur?'

'Here!' said the pig.

'Gander?'

'Here, here, here!' said the gander.

'You sound like three ganders,' muttered Charlotte. 'Why can't you just say "here"? Why do you have to repeat everything?'

'It's my idio-idio-idiosyncrasy,' replied the gander.

'Goose?' said Charlotte.

'Here, here, here!' said the goose. Charlotte glared at her.

'Goslings, one through seven?'

'Bee-bee-bee!' 'Bee-bee-bee!' 'Bee-bee-bee!' 'Bee-bee-bee!' 'Bee-bee-bee!' 'Bee-bee-bee!' 'Bee-bee-bee!' said the goslings.

'This is getting to be quite a meeting,' said Charlotte. 'Anybody would think we had three ganders, three geese, and twenty-one goslings. Sheep?'

'He-aa-aa!' answered the sheep all together.

'Lambs?'

'He-aa-aa!' answered the lambs all together.

'Templeton?'

No answer.

'Well, we are all here except the rat,' said Charlotte. 'I guess we can proceed without him. Now, all of you must have noticed what's been going on around here the last few days. The message I wrote in my web, praising Wilbur, has been received. The Zuckermans have fallen for it, and so has everybody else. Zuckerman thinks Wilbur is an unusual pig, and therefore he won't want to kill him and eat him. I dare say my trick will work and Wilbur's life can be saved.'

'Hurray!' cried everybody.

'Thank you very much,' said Charlotte. 'Now I called this meeting in order to get suggestions. I need new ideas for the web. People are already getting sick of reading the words "SOME PIG!" If anybody can think of another message, or remark, I'll be glad to weave it into the web. Any suggestions for a new slogan?'

'How about "Pig Supreme"?' asked one of the lambs.

'No good,' said Charlotte. 'It sounds like a rich dessert.'

'How about "Terrific, terrific, terrific"?' asked the goose.

49

'Cut that down to one "terrific" and it will do very nicely,' said Charlotte. 'I think "terrific" might impress Zuckerman.'

'But, Charlotte,' said Wilbur, 'I'm *not* terrific.'

'That doesn't make a particle of difference,' replied Charlotte. 'Not a particle. People believe almost anything they see in print. Does anybody here know how to spell "terrific"?'

'I think,' said the gander, 'it's tee double ee double rr double rr double eye double ff double eye double see see see see see.'

The Wolves of Willoughby Chase

JOAN AIKEN

> Sylvia, an orphan, is travelling by steam train to Willoughby Chase to live with her cousin, Bonnie. The only other person in her compartment is a rather odd gentleman, who has fallen asleep.

Presently she grew drowsy and fell into uneasy slumber, but not for long; it was bitterly cold and her feet in their thin shoes felt like lumps of ice. She huddled into her corner and wrapped herself in the green cloak, envying her companion his thick furs and undisturbed repose, and wishing it were ladylike to curl her feet up beneath her on the seat. Unfortunately she knew better than that.

She dreamed, without being really asleep, of arctic seas, of monstrous tunnels through hillsides fringed with icicles. Her travelling companion, who had grown a long tail and a pair of horns, offered her cakes the size of grand pianos and coloured scarlet, blue, and green; when she bit into them she found they were made of snow.

She woke suddenly from one of these dreams to find that the train had stopped with a jerk.

"Oh! What is it? Where are we?" she exclaimed before she could stop herself.

"No need to alarm yourself, miss," said her companion, looking unavailingly out of the black square of window.

"Wolves on the line, most likely – they often have trouble of that kind hereabouts."

"Wolves!" Sylvia stared at him in terror.

"They don't often get into the train, though," he added reassuringly, "Two years ago they managed to climb into the guard's van and eat a pig, and once they got the engine-driver – another had to be sent in a relief-engine – but they don't often catch a passenger, I promise you."

As if in contradiction of his words a sad and sinister howling now arose beyond the windows, and Sylvia, pressing her face against the dark pane, saw that they were passing through a thickly wooded region where snow lay deep on the ground. Across this white carpet she could just discern a ragged multitude pouring, out of which arose, from time to time, this terrible cry. She was almost petrified with fear and sat clutching Annabelle in a cold and trembling hand. At length she summoned up strength to whisper:

"Why don't we go on?"

"Oh, I expect there are too many of 'em on the line ahead," the man answered carelessly. "Can't just push through them, you see – the engine would be derailed in no time, and then we *should* be in a bad way. No, I expect we'll have to wait here till daylight now – the wolves get scared then, you know, and make for home. All that matters is that the driver shan't get eaten in the meantime – he'll keep 'em off by throwing lumps of coal at them I dare say."

"Oh!" Sylvia exclaimed in irrepressible alarm, as a heavy body thudded suddenly against the window, and she had a momentary view of a pointed grey head, red slavering jaws, and pale eyes gleaming with ferocity.

"Oh, don't worry about that," soothed her companion. "They'll keep up that jumping against the windows for hours. They're not much danger, you know, singly; it's only in the whole pack you've got to watch out for 'em."

Sylvia was not much comforted by this. She moved along to the middle of the seat and huddled there, glancing fearfully first to one side and then to the other. The strange man seemed quite undisturbed by the repeated onslaught of the wolves which followed. He took a pinch of snuff, remarked that it was all a great nuisance and they would be late, and composed himself to sleep again.

He had just begun to snore when a discomposing incident occurred. The window beside him, which must have been insecurely fastened, was not proof against the continuous impact of the frenzied and ravenous animals. The catch suddenly slipped, and the window fell open with a crash, its glass shivering into fragments.

Sylvia screamed. Another instant, and a wolf precipitated itself through the aperture thus formed. It turned snarling on the sleeping stranger, who started awake with an oath, and very adroitly flung his cloak over the animal. He then seized one of the shattered pieces of glass lying on the floor and stabbed the imprisoned beast through the cloak. It fell dead.

"Tush," said Sylvia's companion, breathing heavily and passing his hand over his face. "Unexpected – most."

There is more about wolves on pages 96, 98, 100, 102 and 104.

The Tripods

JOHN CHRISTOPHER

> The human race is controlled by monstrous alien Tripods.
> Here, Will is describing a very important day for his friend Jack.

The weather stayed fine until Capping Day. From morning till night people worked in the fields, cutting the grass for hay. There had been so much rain earlier that it stood high and luxuriant, a promise of good winter fodder. The Day itself, of course, was a holiday. After breakfast, we went to church, and the parson preached on the rights and duties of manhood, into which Jack was to enter. Not of womanhood, because there was no girl to be Capped. Jack, in fact, stood alone, dressed in the white tunic which was prescribed. I looked at him, wondering how he was feeling, but whatever his emotions were, he did not show them.

Not even when, the service over, we stood out in the street in front of the church, waiting for the Tripod. The bells were ringing the Capping Peal, but apart from that all was quiet. No one talked or whispered or smiled. It was, we knew, a great experience for everyone who had been Capped. Even the Vagrants came and stood in the same rapt silence. But for us children, the time lagged desperately. And for Jack, apart from everyone, in the middle of the street? I felt for the first time a shiver of fear, in the realization that at the next Capping I would be standing there. I would not be alone, of course, because Henry was to be presented with me. There was not much consolation in that thought.

At last we heard, above the clang of bells, the deep staccato booming in the distance, and there was a kind of sigh from everyone. The booming came nearer and then, suddenly, we could see it over the roofs of the houses to the south: the great hemisphere of gleaming metal rocking through the air above the three articulated legs, several times as high as the church. Its shadow came before it, and fell on us when it halted, two of its legs astride the river and the mill. We waited, and I was shivering in earnest now, unable to halt the tremors that ran through my body.

Sir Geoffrey, the Lord of our Manor, stepped forward and made a small stiff bow in the direction of the Tripod; he was an old man, and could not bend much nor easily. And so one of the enormous burnished tentacles came down, gently and precisely, and its tip curled about Jack's waist, and it lifted him up, up, to where a hole opened like a mouth in the hemisphere, and swallowed him.

In the afternoon there were games, and people moved about the village, visiting, laughing and talking, and the young men and women who were unmarried strolled together in the fields. Then, in the evening, there was the Feast, with tables set up in the street since the weather held fair, and the smell of roast beef mixing with the smells of beer and cyder and lemonade, and all kinds of cakes and puddings. Lamps were hung outside the houses; in the dusk they would be lit, and glow like yellow blossoms along the street. But before the Feast started, Jack was brought back to us.

There was the distant booming first, and the quietness and waiting, and the tread of the gigantic feet, shaking the earth.

The Tripod halted as before, and the mouth opened in the side of the hemisphere, and then the tentacle swept down and carefully set Jack by the place which had been left for him at Sir Geoffrey's right hand. I was a long way away, with the children at the far end, but I could see him clearly. He looked pale, but otherwise his face did not seem any different. The difference was in his white shaved head, on which the darker metal tracery of the Cap stood out like a spider's web. His hair would soon grow again, over and around the metal, and, with thick black hair such as he had, in a few months the Cap would be almost unnoticeable. But it would be there all the same, a part of him now till the day he died.

This, though, was the moment of rejoicing and making merry. He was a man, and tomorrow would do a man's work and get a man's pay. They cut the choicest fillet of beef and brought it to him, with a frothing tankard of ale, and Sir Geoffrey toasted his health and fortune. I forgot my earlier fears, and envied him, and thought how next year I would be there, a man myself.

The Snow-Walker's Son

CATHERINE FISHER

Prologue

The door was the last one in the corridor.

As the flames flickered over it they showed it was barred; a hefty iron chain hung across it, and the mud floor beneath was red with rust that had flaked off in the long years of locking and unlocking.

The keeper hung his lantern on a nail, took the key from a dirty string around his neck, and fitted it into the keyhole. Then he looked behind him.

'Get on with it!' the big man growled. 'Let me see what she keeps in there!'

The keeper grinned; he knew fear when he heard it. With both hands he turned the key, then tugged out the red chain in a shower of rust and pushed the door. It opened, just a fraction. Darkness and a damp smell oozed through the black slit.

He stepped well back, handed the stranger the lantern, and jerked his head. He had no tongue to speak with; she'd made sure he kept her secrets.

The stranger hesitated; a draught moved his hair and he gazed back up the stone passageway as if he longed suddenly for warmth and light. And from what I've heard, the keeper thought, you won't be seeing much of those ever again.

Then the man held up the lantern and pushed the door. The keeper watched his face intently in the red glow, and his great hand, as it clutched a luck-stone that swung at his neck. The man went in, slowly. The door closed.

Outside, the keeper waited, listening. No sound came out of the room and he dared not go too close. For six years now he had locked it and unlocked it, letting in the witch Gudrun and the sly old dwarf she brought with her. No one else in all that time – until today, this gruff red-beard.

For six years he had left food at the door and taken it away half eaten; had heard rustles and movements and had never looked in. But there had been that night, nearly a year ago now, when halfway up the corridor he had looked back, and in the dimness seen that hand, thin as a claw, lifting the platter.

Suddenly the door opened; he stiffened, his hand on his knife. The big man was there, carrying something heavy, wrapped in old bearskins. He cradled it with both arms; whatever it was moved in the heavy folds against his shoulder. It made a low sound, wordless and strange.

The man had changed. His face was pale, his voice quiet. 'Tell her,' he muttered through his teeth, 'that her secret is safe with me. I'll keep it better than she did.'

Shoving the keeper aside, he strode through the flames and shadows of the stone tunnel.

The keeper waited; waited until the echoes of distant chains and gates were still. Then, furtively, he slid his lantern around the door and looked into the room.

He saw a small cell, with one window high up in the wall, icicles hanging from its sill; a low bed; straw; a fireplace full of ashes. He stepped in, warily. There were a few scraps of food on the floor, but nothing to give any sign of what had been here.

It was only when he turned to go that his eyes caught the patterns: the rows and rows of strange, whirling spirals scrawled on the damp wall next to the bed.

Chapter 1

*Young and alone on a long road,
Once I lost my way:
Rich I felt when I found another...*

The Hall was empty.

Jessa edged inside and began to wander idly about, pulling the thick furred collar of her coat up around her face. She was early.

It had been a bitter night. The snow had blown in under the door and spread across the floor. A pool of wine that someone had spilt under the table was frozen to a red slab. She nudged it with her foot; solid as glass. Even the spiders were dead on their webs; the thin nets shook in the draught.

She walked to the great pillar of oak that grew up through the middle of the Hall. It was heavily carved with old runes and magic signs, but over them all, obliterating them, was a newer cutting: a contorted snake that twisted itself down in white spirals. She brushed the frost off it with her gloved fingers. The snake was Gudrun's sign. A witch's sign.

The December Rose

LEON GARFIELD

There was a boy up the chimney, but only God and Mister Roberts knew exactly where. How God came by His knowledge was, of course, a holy mystery; and how Mister Roberts came by his was almost as wonderful an affair. He'd only to lay his ear against a wall, medically so to speak, as if it was a wheezy chest, and it was enough! Leaving a black ear behind, he'd rush to the nearest fireplace, insert his head, and bellow upwards: 'I knows yer, Barnacle! I knows ye're just squattin' up there, a-pickin' of yer nose! Git on with yer sweepin', lad, or I'll light a fire and scorch yer to a black little twig! So help me,' he would add, for he was a devout man, 'God!'

Up and up the dreadful threat would fly, booming and echoing through all the narrow, dark and twisty flues, until it found out Barnacle, exactly as Mister Roberts had divined, squatting in some sooty nook and, if there was room enough to move his arms, a-picking of his nose.

'I knows yer – yer - yer … Git on – on – on – on …scorch yer – yer – yer …'

Barnacle, neatly wedged in an elbow of broken brick, went on with picking his nose and waiting for 'God!'

His proper name was Absalom Brown, but his owner, Mister Roberts, called him Barnacle on account of his amazing powers of holding on. He could attach himself to the inside of a flue by finger- and toe-holds at which even a fly might have blinked. It was a real gift, and the only one he had. Otherwise he was a child of darkness, no better, as Mister Roberts often had cause to shout, than a animal.

'So help me, God – God – God – God!' came Mister Roberts's voice, and Barnacle began brushing away at the soot, and dislodged a piece of brickwork for good measure. He heard it go bumping and rattling down until at last it clanged to a stop against the iron bars of a distant grate.

'Watch it, lad – lad – lad – lad!'

'Watch it, 'e says,' marvelled Barnacle, who was as tight in blackness as a stone in a plum. 'An' wot wiv, might I arst?'

Eyes weren't any help, as it was as dark outside his head as it was within; and anyway he was too bone-idle to open them. It was his fingers, elbows and knees that told him where he was, and it was his nose that told him where he was going, and, most important of all, it was his ears that warned him of what was to come: either the wrath of Mister Roberts or a sudden fall of stinking, choking soot that was always heralded by a tiny whispering click.

Cautiously he eased himself up the flue, clearing the soot as he went, partly with his brush and partly with the spiky stubble that grew out of his head. Once he'd had a cap, but he'd lost it in his infancy, trying to swipe at a pigeon as he'd come out of the top of a chimney-pot. He'd cried bitterly over the loss, not of the cap but of the brass badge on the front of it that had proclaimed him to be a boy of importance, a climbing boy belonging to a master sweep.

Limericks

There was an old fellow from Tyre,
Who constantly sat on the fire.
When asked 'Are you hot?'
He said 'Certainly not.
I'm James Winterbotham, Esquire.'

There was a young lady of Twickenham,
Whose boots were too tight to walk quickenham;
She bore them a while,
But at last, at a stile,
She pulled them both off and was sickenham.

Zebra

MAL PEET

**The dry zebra sees
her camouflage dissolve in
wet perplextasy.**

There is another poem in haiku form on page 88.

Two Cinquains

Adelaide Crapsey

November Night

Listen…..
With faint dry sound,
Like steps of passing ghosts,
The leaves, frost-crisped, break from the trees
And fall.

The Warning

Just now
Out of the strange
Still dusk – as strange, as still –
A white moth flew. Why am I grown
So cold?

Calligram

GUILLAUME APOLLINAIRE (TRANSLATED BY O. BERNARD)

The sky's as blue and black as ink
My eyes drown in it and sink

Darkness a shell whines over me
I write this under a willow tree

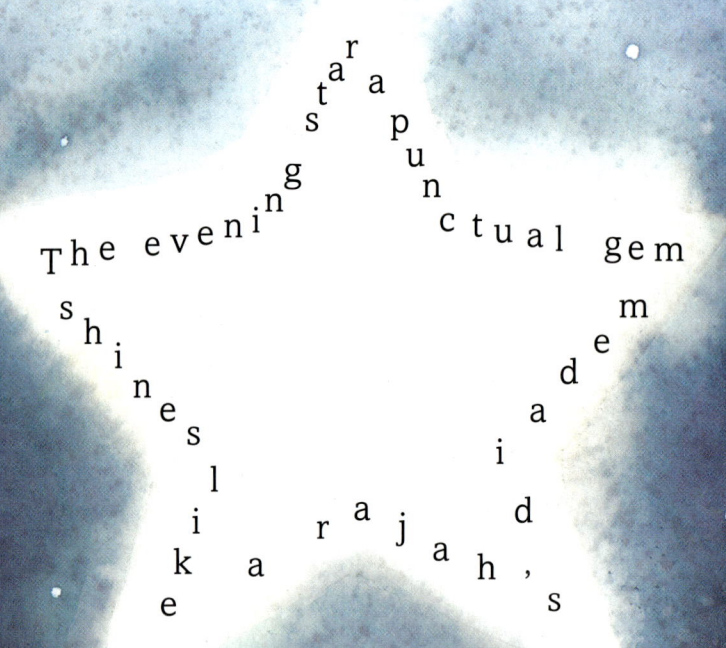

The evening star a punctual gem shines like a rajah's diademe

Two Riddles

JOHN MOLE

Who, Sir, am I?

Who, sir am I?
For a start, I hate sunshine
And deserve the penalty –
To be swallowed with good wine.
Miserable slitherer,
Landlubberly crustacean;
The French eat me, sir.
They are a wise nation!

snail

I am the Shame beneath a Carpet

I am the shame beneath a carpet.
No one comes to sweep me off my feet.

Abandoned rooms and unread books collect me.
Sometimes I dance like particles of light.

My legions thicken on each window pane,
A gathering of dusk, perpetual gloom,

And when at last the house has fallen,
I am the cloud left hanging in the air.

dust

An Attempt at Unrhymed Verse

WENDY COPE

People tell you all the time,
Poems do not have to rhyme.
It's often better if they don't
And I'm determined this one won't.
                        Oh dear.

Never mind, I'll start again,
Busy, busy with my pen… cil.
I can do it, if I try,
Easy, peasy, pudding and gherkins.

Writing verse is so much fun,
Cheering as the summer weather,
Makes you feel alert and bright,
'Specially when you get it more or less the way you want it.

My Last Nature Walk

ADRIAN MITCHELL

I strode among the clumihacken
Where scrubble nudges to the barfter
Till I whumped into, hidden in the bracken,
A groolted after-laughter-rafter.

(For milty Wah-Zohs do guffaw
Upon a laughter-rafter perch.
But after laughter they balore
Unto a second beam to gurch.)
Yet here was but one gollamonce!
I glumped upon the after-laughter-rafter.
Where was its other-brother? Oh! My bonce!
The Wah-Zohs blammed it with a laughter-rafter.

Moral: Never gamble on a bramble ramble.

Glossary:
clumihacken – the old stalks of wild Brussels sprouts
scrubble – unusually tall moss, often scuffed
the barfter – the height at which low clouds cruise
to whump – to bump into, winding oneself in the process
groolted – cunningly engraved with the portraits of barbers
milty – clean but mean-minded
Wah-Zohs' – French birds, sometimes spelt Oiseaux
to balore – to hover fatly downwards
to gurch – to recover from cheerfulness
gollamonce – a thing that is sought for, for no reason
to glump – to glump
to blam – to shonk on the cloddle

'You're Right,' Said Grandad

JOAN POULSON

I went round to help him
the day he moved
it was an upstairs flat
this old one he had
he'd lived there
with Gran
for twenty-nine years
they told him
it was time
he had a move.

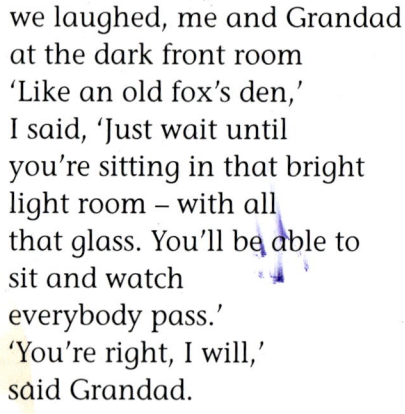

we laughed, me and Grandad
at the dark front room
'Like an old fox's den,'
I said, 'Just wait until
you're sitting in that bright
light room – with all
that glass. You'll be able to
sit and watch
everybody pass.'
'You're right, I will,'
said Grandad.

we laughed, me and Grandad
at the garden round the back.
'Like a jungle, at its best,'
I said. 'Just wait until
you're resting in your
new place. No more
hacking-out
a deckchair space.
No weeds annoying you.
There'll be plenty
company for you, too.

They'll sit outside
the people from
the other bungalows
sit on the benches
chat with you.'
'You're right, they will,'
said Grandad.

we laughed, me and Grandad
at his rickety old shed.
'Like something from
a horror film!' I said.
'You'll be much better off
without it. And didn't
the doctor tell you
all that sawdust
wasn't good, got on your chest?
And we've all got wooden stools
and things, enough to last
a lifetime, anyway.
Our Sheryll really loved
that box you made her.
All those different
colours, different woods.
Dad says you've been a
first-rate craftsman
in your time.'
'He's right, I have,'
said Grandad.
'Yes, I have.'

Should prisoners have TV sets in their cells?

Yes, says Jerry, an ex-prisoner. **No**, says Simon, a prison officer.

JERRY What prison does, obviously, is cut you off from the outside world. But most prisoners leave prison eventually, and a lot of them find it very difficult. TV keeps you in touch with the outside world. It helps you adjust to real life again. Many prisoners are more or less illiterate – they can't keep in touch with the world by reading newspapers or books.

SIMON I'm glad you mention illiteracy, because it's a key issue. You'd probably agree that many people are in jail because they have educational problems. I think that we should be spending every available penny on education, rather than tellies. It's a question of priorities.

JERRY If society was really serious about cutting crime, we'd spend much more money on prison education, agreed. But going back to isolation, prisoners spend at least 15 hours a day banged up in their cells. Often 23 hours a day. That's what leads to frustration, anger, violence. There are a lot of disturbed people in prison, and being pent up in cells, bored rigid, makes them worse. TV in cells would take the edge off that. It would lead to a more peaceful prison environment, and you've got to be in favour of that, haven't you?

SIMON That's a bit naive, I think. Violent people are violent people whether they watch telly or not. And there's plenty of violence on TV – are you sure it's good for disturbed people to watch that stuff? But that's not the main point. Of course it's bad that prisoners are locked up for hours on end. I'd like to see more time for exercise, for training, for developing personal skills, for contact with the outside world, for conversation, for all those things that can rehabilitate prisoners. I'm sorry to come back to money again, but it's the key issue. We haven't got the resources to provide all those things.

JERRY No, which is why putting TV sets in cells is a sensible option; TVs aren't very expensive. Anyway, TV can do some of the things you mention: there's intelligent conversation on TV, there's good educational stuff, there's informational programmes.

SIMON Oh come on, Jerry: are you telling me that prisoners are going to sit around watching documentaries and nature programmes? I think not.

JERRY Not all of us, not all the time, no. But being a criminal doesn't necessarily mean that you're ignorant, you know.

SIMON Fair comment. But some prisoners *do* have tellies in their cells. These are prisoners who have a record of good behaviour; they've *earned* the right to have them. If we gave *all* prisoners TV sets, they wouldn't have that incentive for good behaviour. Telly for everyone would make behaviour worse, not better.

JERRY There's no proof of that, of course. But what you're saying is that you're treating prisoners like children – giving them sweeties for being good. Surely prison should be about making prisoners into better people. And the only way to do that is to treat them with a little respect.

SIMON Yes, prisons are in the business of trying to make prisoners better people. You seem to be arguing that watching telly makes you a better person; do you really believe that?

A Guide to the U.N. Convention

WHAT OTHER RIGHTS DOES THE CONVENTION GIVE CHILDREN?
CIVIL AND POLITICAL RIGHTS

These are to do with children being respected as people and having a right to take part in society, and to be involved in matters which are important to them.

Name and nationality at birth
All children have a right to a name when they are born and to be able to become a citizen of a particular country (*Article 7*).

Freedom of expression
Children have the right to express what they think and feel so long as by doing so they do not break the law or affect other people's rights (*Article 13*).

Freedom of thought, conscience and religion
Parents have a duty to give guidance but children have the right to choose their own religion, and to have their own views as soon as they are able to decide for themselves (*Article 14*).

Meeting other people
Children have the right to join organisations and to take part in meetings, and peaceful demonstrations, so long as they are not against the law and that by doing so children do not affect other people's rights (*Article 15*).

Convention on the Rights of the Child

Article 13
1. The child shall have the right to freedom of expression; this right shall include freedom to seek, receive and impart information and ideas of all kinds, regardless of frontiers, either orally, in writing or in print, in the form of art, or through any other media of the child's choice.
2. The exercise of this right may be subject to certain restrictions, but these shall only be such as are provided by law and are necessary:
   a) For respect of the rights or reputations of others; or
   b) For the protection of national security or of public order (ordre public), or of public health or morals.

Article 14
1. States Parties shall respect the right of the child to freedom of thought, conscience and religion.
2. States Parties shall respect the rights and duties of the parents and, when applicable, legal guardians, to provide direction to the child in the exercise of his or her right in a manner consistent with the evolving capacities of the child.
3. Freedom to manifest one's religion or beliefs may be subject only to such limitations as are prescribed by law and are necessary to protect public safety, order, health or morals, or the fundamental rights and freedoms of others.

Article 15
1. States Parties recognize the rights of the child to freedom of association and to freedom of peaceful assembly.
2. No restrictions may be placed on the exercise of these rights other than those imposed in conformity with the law and which are necessary in a democratic society in the interests of national security or public safety, public order (ordre public), the protection of public health or morals or the protection of the rights and freedoms of others.

Flour Babies

ANNE FINE

> Class 4C have been set a science project. The boys have each been given a small sack of flour to care for as if it were a baby.

Simon sat across the kitchen table from his flour baby and gave her a poke.

The flour baby fell over.

'Ha!' Simon scoffed. 'Can't even sit up yet!'

He set the flour baby up again, and gave her another poke. Again, she fell over.

'Not very good at standing up for yourself, are you?' Simon taunted, setting her up again.

The flour baby fell over backwards this time, off the table into the dog basket.

'Blast!'

'You mustn't swear in front of it,' Simon's mother said. 'You'll set it a terrible example.'

Simon reached down to scoop the flour baby off Macpherson's cushion, and picked the dog's hairs off her frock.

'Not *it*,' he reproved his mum in turn. '*Her*.'

She was definitely a her. Definitely. Some of the flour babies Mr Cartright had handed out that morning could have been one or the other. It wasn't clear. But not the one that landed in Simon's lap.

'Catch, Dozy! Aren't you supposed to be one of the school's sporting heroes? Wake up!'

She was *sweet*. She was dressed in a frilly pink bonnet and a pink nylon frock, and carefully painted on her sacking were luscious sexy round eyes fringed with fluttering lashes.

Robin Foster, beside him, was jealous instantly.

'How come you get one with eyes? Mine's just plain sacking. Do you want to swap?'

Simon tightened his grip round his flour baby.

'No. She's mine. You paint eyes on your own if you want them.'

'And yours has clothes!' He turned to yell at Mr Cartright, who was just coming to the end of tossing bags of flour round the room. 'Sir! Sir! Sime's dolly has got a frock and a bonnet and eyes and everything. And mine's got nothing. It's not fair.'

'If every parent who had a baby who was a bit lacking sent it back,' Mr Cartright said, 'this classroom would be practically empty. Sit down and be quiet.'

He heaved himself up on the desk, and started reading the rules of the experiment.

FLOUR BABIES

1. The flour babies must be kept clean and dry at all times. All fraying, staining and leakage of stuffing will be taken very seriously indeed.
2. Flour babies will be put on the official scales twice a week to

check for any weight loss that might indicate casual neglect or maltreatment, or any weight gain that might indicate tampering or damp.
3. No flour baby may be left unattended at any time, night or day. If you *must* be out of sight of your flour baby, even for a short time, a responsible babysitter must be arranged.
4. You must keep a Baby Book, and write in it daily. Each entry should be no shorter than three full sentences, and no longer than five pages.
5. Certain persons (who shall not be named until the experiment is over) shall make it their business to check on the welfare of the flour babies and the keeping of the above rules. These people may be parents, other pupils, or members of staff or the public.

He looked up.
'That's it.'

> There is more about learning to care for babies on pages 40 and 41. Other pieces by Anne Fine are on pages 79 and 82.

Step by Wicked Step

ANNE FINE

Ralph reached above his head to switch on the light.

'Mine's not a tale of woe,' he said, peeling the top slice of bread back from his sandwich to peer suspiciously at the filling. 'But it is *complicated*, so you have to pay attention.' He laid down his sandwich and started to count on his fingers. 'I have two brothers, two half-brothers, one half-sister, three stepbrothers, one stepsister, three stepmothers – that's two old ones and one at the moment – one stepfather, two stepgrannies and one stepgrandpa that I know, and some more that I don't know. And, any day now, when Flora has her baby, I'm going to have another half-sister.'

He paused, looking puzzled, as if he'd surprised himself by ending up on the wrong finger.

'Oh, yes!' he said. 'And I have a mum and dad.'

Satisfied, he carried on.

'On Mondays and Thursdays I go directly to Dad's place after school. And every other weekend Mum drives me there, unless it's the third Saturday in the month, when she has her hair trimmed. On that day my stepdad drives me. He's called Howard.'

He looked around, as if to check they were still paying attention.

'On Tuesdays, Wednesdays and Fridays, on the other hand, I go straight home to Mum's, unless my dad can't manage the following weekend (if it's his). Then I'm supposed to go to his house to make up, unless it's Wednesday. You see, I have orchestra on Thursday morning, and my horn's never at Dad's house unless we're close to a concert, with Sunday rehearsals, and I was at Dad's house on the Sunday before.'

'Stop there,' said Pixie. 'I'm already lost.'

'How can you ever remember where you're going?' demanded Claudia. 'You'd have to be a genius to work it out.'

'I used to get it wrong a lot,' Ralph told them cheerfully. 'I'd keep arriving at one house or the other and find no one there. I wouldn't know whether to sit on the doorstep and wait, or go back to the other house. But then they bought me new lunchboxes: two with Mickey Mouse on the side, and two more with Dumbo.'

'How did that help?'

'Easy,' Ralph said. '*D* for Dumbo and Dad, and *M* for

Mickey and Mum. If I wasn't sure which house I was aiming for, I looked at my lunchbox.'

'Why *four*?'

'A pair for each house,' said Ralph. 'And even then they'd sometimes both end up in the same place, and Mum or Annabel would have to stick a label on the side saying 'Not Mickey, Dumbo,' or 'Not Dumbo, Mickey'.'

There are other pieces by Anne Fine on pages 76 and 82.

Goggle Eyes

Anne Fine

> Kitty's mum has a new boyfriend, and Kitty doesn't like him one bit. She calls him 'Goggle Eyes'. Here, Goggle Eyes has dared to enter Kitty's room to find out why the heating isn't working.

He slotted himself in sideways, and peered through the gloom.

'Why is it so dark in here?' he asked. 'Why haven't you opened your curtains?'

I stepped back, tripping on wires from my computer and my hair crimpers tangled all over the floor.

'I haven't had time yet.'

'Time? It's practically evening. If you don't open them soon, it will be time to close them again.'

I ignored him. He lifted a foot and slid it gingerly between my plastic bags full of spare wools and some dirty old tea cups. You could tell he was trying really hard not to tread on the clothes that

I hadn't had time to hang up yet. But there was not much actual carpet showing, and he tipped a cereal bowl with his heel. Luckily Floss had drunk most of the milk, and the cornflakes had dried up.

He flung the curtains open. Light flooded the room.

There was stunned silence, then:

'Dear gods!' he whispered softly in some awe. 'Designer compost!'

He gazed about him in amazement. And it did look a bit slummy, I admit. Blackened banana skins don't look too nasty dropped in a waste paper basket, but when you see them spread on your crumpled bedclothes, coated with cat hairs, they can be a bit off-putting. And the tops were off most of the make-up and hair stuff. And the playing cards would have looked neater in a pile. And if my dresser drawers had been pushed in, none of my underwear would have been spilling on the floor.

He stopped to pick up a mug with two inches of stone cold coffee inside it, and a layer of thick green scum over the top.

'Interesting,' he said. 'Bit of a rarity, this particular mould.'

'I think you mentioned an airlock in our pipes,' I said coldly.

Notice that? Not *the* pipes. *Our* pipes. I always hoped that if I managed to make him sound enough like a trespasser in our house, he might go away. It never worked.

'Oh, yes.'

He made a space for the coffee cup on my desk, between my furry slippers and a large tin of cat food I must have brought up from downstairs one night when Floss seemed hungry. There was a metallic clink as he put down the cup. We both heard it. He brushed a couple of letters from my dad aside, and picked up something lying underneath.

Scissors.

'Kitty,' he said. 'Are these the scissors your mother spent three days searching for last week?'

I flushed. I knew that he'd been at her side each time she pleaded with me to scour my room one more time, because her precious sharp hair-cutting scissors couldn't have been anywhere else but there. He'd heard me *insisting* I had looked under absolutely everything, thoroughly, twice, and they were most definitely not there.

He laid the scissors down beside the wrench with a sigh, and turned away. Brushing aside a tell-tale nest of crinkly wrappers from the last box of chocolates he'd brought to the house, he knelt down on the floor.

'Do you mind if I prise a few of these odd socks out from behind your radiator?' he asked politely. 'Principles of convection, you understand.'

'*I'll* get them out.'

I wouldn't have seemed so keen to cooperate, but you know how it is when someone starts rooting around the more impenetrable areas of your bedroom. You never know if they're going to turn up something so embarrassing you'll *die* of shame.

As I reached in the top of the radiator, he tapped the bottom sharply. Two shrivelled apple cores shot out.

He frowned.

'That pinging noise,' he said. 'It's making me just a wee bit suspicious.'

I thought he meant my radiator must have sprung a leak. But when he'd fished behind the metal casing with a stick he found in my *Stop Trident* collection, he managed to bring up four house keys tangled together with string.

Dangling them from his finger, Exhibit A, he looked at me gravely.

'Now these will set your mother's mind at rest,' he remarked. 'She's been wondering what on earth happened to all the door keys.'

He tapped the radiator again, a little harder. Another apple core shot out, stuck to a chocolate that I didn't like much, and there was a rich-sounding gurgle as water welled freely along the pipes for the first time in days.

'There.' He sat back on his heels. 'I think that might well be the problem solved.'

Brushing green eye-glitter from the knees of his trousers, he stood and took one more slow, marvelling look around my room. His eyes, I noticed, came to rest on my pot plant.

'Fascinating,' he said. 'Look at it. No water. No fresh air. No sunlight. And still it lives.'

'Is that it?' I asked coldly. 'Are you finished?'

He turned and pulled the door back as far as it would go against my heap of English books.

'Miss Kitty Killin,' he said admiringly, edging as best he could through the narrow gap. 'The only girl in the whole world who can make litter out of literature!'

Before I could stick out my tongue at him, he had gone.

There are other pieces by Anne Fine on pages 76 and 79.

Caterpillar

Norman MacCaig

He stands on the suckers under his tail,
stretches forward and puts down
his six legs. Then he brings up
the sucker under his tail, making
a beautiful loop.

That's his way of walking. He makes
a row of upside-down U's
along the rib of a leaf. He is as green
as it.

The ways of walking! – horse, camel,
snail, me, crab, rabbit –
all inventing a way of journeying
till they become like the green caterpillar
that now stands on his tail
on the very tip of the leaf and sways, sways
like a tiny charmed snake,
groping in empty space for a foothold
where none is, where there is no
foothold at all.

There are more poems by Norman MacCaig on pages 20 and 87.

By the Canal, Early March

NORMAN MACCAIG

The snow is trash now and the blackbirds sing
A gold and blue day trying to be Spring.
A gray sludge fringes the canal where swans,
Almost as gray, surge by, their wings like tents,
Hissing with love between the tenements.

Posters are peeled that once hung in the air
Their vulgar summers; but drab windows stare
Winking and blinking at the boisterous sun.
Low, the brown water breaks in glass and high
The tall mill cracks its smokelash in the sky.

And everything is headlong, rushing through
Spaces of sun and sky, their gold and blue,
Towards that still certain time when buds all break
And sparrows quarrel in the dust and men
Lounge their ways home and swans are white again.

There are more poems by Norman MacCaig on pages 20 and 86.
Other poems about the seasons are on pages 88 and 90.

January to December

PATRICIA BEER

The warm cows have gone
From the fields where grass stands up
Dead-alive like steel.

Unexpected sun
Probes the house as if someone
Had left the lights on.

Novel no longer
Snowdrops melt in the hedge, drain
Away into spring.

The heron shining
Works his way up the bright air
Above the river.

Earth dries. The sow basks
Flat out with her blue-black young,
Ears over their eyes.

The early lambs, still
Fleecy, look bulkier now
Than their mothers.

In this valley full
Of birdsong, the gap closes
Behind the cuckoo.

Fields of barley glimpsed
Through trees shine out like golden
Windows in winter.

Though nothing has changed –
The sun is even hotter –
Death is in the air.

Long shadows herald
Or dog every walker
In the cut-back lanes.

A crop of mist grows
Softly in the valley, lolls
Over the strawstacks.

Meadows filmed across
With rain stare up at winter
Heardening in the hills.

There are more poems about the seasons on pages 87 and 90. There is another haiku poem on page 64.

It's Spring, It's Spring!

Kit Wright

It's spring, it's spring –

when everyone sits round a roaring fire
telling ghost stories!

It's spring, it's spring –

when everyone sneaks into everyone else's yard
and bashes up their snowman!

It's spring, it's spring –

when the last dead leaves fall from the trees
and Granny falls off your toboggan!

It's spring, it's spring –

when you'd give your right arm
for a steaming hot bowl of soup!

It's spring, it's spring –

when you'd give your right leg
not to be made to wash up after Christmas dinner!

It's spring, it's spring –

isn't it?

There are more poems about the seasons on pages 87 and 88.

A Fly

Ruth Dallas

If I could
See this fly
With unprejudiced eye,
I should see his body
Was metallic blue – no,
Peacock blue.
His wings are a frosty puff;
His legs fine wire.
He even has a face,
I notice.
And he breathes as I do.

There are more poems about flies on pages 92, 93 and 94.

The Fly

WILLIAM BLAKE

Little Fly,
Thy summer's play
My thoughtless hand
Has brushed away.

Am not I
A fly like thee?
Or art not thou
A man like me?

For I dance,
And drink, and sing,
Till some blind hand
Shall brush my wing.

If thought is life
And strength and breath,
And the want
Of thought is death;

Then am I
A happy fly,
If I live
Or if I die.

There are more poems about flies on pages 91, 93 and 94.

House Flies

N. M. Bodecker

What makes
common house flies
trying
is
that they keep
multiflieing.

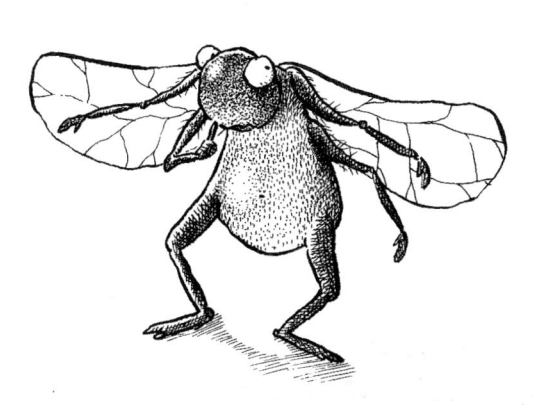

The Fly

Ogden Nash

God in his wisdom made the fly
And then forgot to tell us why.

There are more poems about flies on pages 91, 92 and 94.

U.S. Flies in Hamburgers *

ROGER MCGOUGH

If you go down the High Street today
You'll be sure of a big surprise.
When you order your favourite burger
With a milkshake and regular fries.

For the secret is out
I tell you no lies
They've stopped using beef
In favour of FLIES.

FLIES, FLIES, big juicy FLIES,
FLIES as American as apple pies.

Horseflies, from Texas, as big as your thumb
Are sautéed with onions and served in a bun.

Free-range bluebottles, carefully rinsed
Are smothered in garlic, and painlessly minced.

* Newspaper headline referring to hamburgers being airlifted to U.S. Marines.

Black-eyed bees with stings intact
Add a zesty zing, and that's a fact.

Colorado beetles, ants from Kentucky,
Rhode Island roaches, and if you're unlucky

Baltimore bedbugs (and even horrider)
Leeches as squashy as peaches from Florida.

FLIES, FLIES, big juicy FLIES,
FLIES as American as mom's apple pies.

It's lovely down in MacDingles today
But if you don't fancy flies
Better I'd say to keep well away
Stay home and eat Birds' Eyes.

There are more poems about flies on pages 91, 92 and 93.

Wolf

GILLIAN CROSS

> Cassy has met Lyall and Robert, who put on shows in schools. Their next show is going to be about wolves. They have gone to a zoo, very early in the morning, to record the sound of wolves' 'singing'.

Suddenly, from round the corner, came a whine followed by a long, low moan that prickled the hairs on her neck. She began to scramble up, but Lyall was ready for that. One of his huge hands grabbed the back of her neck, forcing her down again, and he put a finger fiercely to his lips.

The moan broke off and started again, not alone this time. Other voices joined in, but they did not keep together. The pitches shifted constantly, each one avoiding all the others. Chords and discords formed and dissolved and formed anew in strange, mournful patterns.

Cassy swallowed and sat up straight. The sound wasn't singing, but it caught at her ears like rough music, with a ragged, irregular harmony.

As the moans grew higher and shorter, Lyall let go of her hand and began to crawl towards the corner. Robert followed, grinning at Cassy and beckoning her until she crept into the space beside Lyall.

Now they could see round the corner, into the wolf enclosure. The six wolves were standing in a circle on top of the mound, facing outwards. Their muzzles were lifted to the sky and their eyes were narrowed, ecstatically, as they howled. Cassy dug her fingernails into the palms of her hands, willing them not to stop. She wanted the beautiful, inhuman noise to go on for ever.

But, one by one, the voices died away until the last one drew out its final, solitary howl. Then that last wolf, too, dropped its head and trotted slowly from the mound.

Cassy realized that she was trembling.

Lyall took two quick steps to the tape recorder and switched it off. Then he turned and grinned triumphantly. 'There! Did you guess what we were waiting for, Cassy?'

She shook her head, because she couldn't speak yet.

'And wasn't it better like that? When you don't know what you're hearing – you really *hear* it!'

'I thought …'. Her voice cracked but she forced it back to steadiness. 'I thought they only did that at night. At the full moon.'

Robert nodded. 'That's why we didn't tell you. We didn't want you to expect something out of a horror film.'

There is more about wolves on pages 51, 98, 100, 102 and 104.

White Fang

JACK LONDON

For two days the she-wolf and One Eye hung about the Indian camp. He was worried and apprehensive, yet the camp lured his mate and she was loath to depart. But when, one morning, the air was rent with the report of a rifle close at hand, and a bullet smashed against a tree trunk several inches from One Eye's head, they hesitated no more, but went off on a long, swinging lope that put quick miles between them and the danger.

They did not go far – a couple of days' journey. The she-wolf's need to find the thing for which she searched had now become imperative. She was getting very heavy, and could run but slowly. Once, in the pursuit of a rabbit, which she ordinarily would have caught with ease, she gave over and lay down and rested. One Eye came to her; but when he touched her neck gently with his muzzle she snapped at him with such quick fierceness that he tumbled over backwards and cut a ridiculous figure in his effort to escape her teeth. Her temper was now shorter than ever; but he had become more patient than ever and more solicitous.

And then she found the thing for which she sought. It was a few miles up a small stream that in the summer time flowed into the Mackenzie, but that then was frozen over and frozen down to its rocky bottom – a dead stream of solid white from source to mouth. The she-wolf was trotting wearily along, her mate well in advance, when she came upon the overhanging, high claybank. She turned aside and trotted over to it. The wear and tear of spring storms and melting snows had underwashed the bank and in one place had made a small cave out of a narrow fissure.

She paused at the mouth of the cave and looked the wall over carefully. Then, on one side and the other, she ran along the base of the wall to where its abrupt bulk merged from the softer-lined landscape. Returning to the cave, she entered its narrow mouth. For a short three feet she was compelled to crouch, then the walls widened and rose higher in a little round chamber nearly six feet in diameter. The roof barely cleared her head. It was dry and cosy. She inspected it with painstaking care, while One Eye, who had returned, stood in the entrance and patiently watched her. She dropped her head, with her nose to the ground and directed towards a point near to her closely bunched feet, and around this point she circled several times; then, with a tired sigh that was almost a grunt, she curled her body in, relaxed her legs, and dropped down, her head toward the entrance.

One Eye, with pointed, interested ears, laughed at her, and beyond, outlined against the white light, she could see the brush of his tail waving good-naturedly. Her own ears, with a snuggling movement, laid their sharp points backward and down against the head for a moment, while her mouth opened and her tongue lolled peaceably out, and in this way she expressed that she was pleased and satisfied.

There is more about wolves on pages 51, 96, 100, 102 and 104.

White Wolf

Henrietta Branford

We travelled slowly. She stopped to dig at every empty burrow, peer into each abandoned beaver lodge, examine and explore each hillside, cave and rock pile. We stopped one morning, climbed a rocky outcrop and looked around. To the north was empty space with just a few stands of birch and poplar and some willow here and there. To the south, back where we had come from, the tops of the trees looked as though you could walk on them. Not-Much nosed around while I rested until she found an old fox burrow, its entrance well hidden by matted, trailing bearberry. Further down the hill, where a stand of aspen was just turning green for springtime, a trickle of water splashed off down the valley.

The earth was soft and the digging was easy. Not-Much started to enlarge the burrow. She dug out a bed for us and beyond that, further into the hillside, a separate small chamber. Then she sent me away. I spent a few days hunting and trotted back up the hill to our den one evening at dusk. I paused at the entrance and looked back down the valley. The smell of rain blew up from the south.

I stuck my nose into the burrow and snuffed Not-Much's good warm smell. Not-Much – and something else. Young, soft and sweet. Three cubs. Not-Much had licked them free of their small sacks, chewed through each cord and fed and cleaned each cub.

Now they lay sleeping, pillowed against the soft fur of her belly – two little dogs and a bitch.

Not-Much looked up without lifting her muzzle from her forepaws. Her eyes shone in the gloom of the chamber. We touched noses, I nuzzled her face and neck, picking up the slight traces of sweat and blood she had not yet licked off. I cleaned her thoroughly from nose to tail and back again. When she was comfortable I slipped back out to fetch a hare I'd left near by. She nosed it politely but was too tired to eat so I took it back out and buried it for later.

Not-Much slept all night with the cubs, while I lay at the mouth of the den keeping watch. I saw the stars swing round the sky, heard owls hunting down the valley, saw the moon rise and set. Now and then I sang quietly to myself for the joy of hearing my own voice calling through the large and lonely space that was my home.

There is more about wolves on pages 51, 96, 98, 102 and 104.

The Jungle Book

RUDYARD KIPLING

'Something is coming up hill,' said Mother Wolf, twitching one ear. 'Get ready.'

The bushes rustled a little in the thicket, and Father Wolf dropped with his haunches under him, ready for his leap. Then, if you had been watching, you would have seen the most wonderful thing in the world – the wolf checked in mid-spring. He made his bound before he saw what it was he was jumping at, and then he tried to stop himself. The result was that he shot up straight into the air for four or five feet, landing almost where he left ground.

'Man!' he snapped. 'A man's cub. Look!'

Directly in front of him, holding on by a low branch, stood a naked brown baby who could just walk – as soft and as dimpled a little atom as ever came to a wolf's cave at night. He looked up into Father Wolf's face and laughed.

'Is that a man's cub?' said Mother Wolf. 'I have never seen one. Bring it here.'

A wolf accustomed to moving his own cubs can, if necessary, mouth an egg without breaking it, and though Father Wolf's jaws closed right on the child's back not a tooth even scratched the skin, as he laid it down among the cubs.

'How little! How naked, and – how bold!' said Mother Wolf, softly. The baby was pushing his way between the cubs to get close to the warm hide.

'Ahai! He is taking his meal with the others. And so this is a man's cub. Now, was there ever a wolf that could boast of a man's cub among her children?'

'I have heard now and again of such a thing, but never in our Pack or in my time,' said Father Wolf. 'He is altogether without hair, and I could kill him with a touch of my foot. But see, he looks up and is not afraid.'

There is more about wolves on pages 51, 96, 98, 100 and 104.

A Night with a Wolf

BAYARD TAYLOR

High up on the lonely mountains,
Where the wild men watched and waited;
Wolves in the forest, and bears in the bush,
And I on my path belated.

The rain and the night together
Came down, and the wind came after,
Bending the props of the pine-tree roof,
And snapping many a rafter.

I crept along in the darkness,
Stunned, and bruised, and blinded;
Crept to a fir with thick-set boughs,
And a sheltering rock behind it.

There, from the blowing and raining,
Crouching, I sought to hide me.
Something rustled; two green eyes shone;
And a wolf lay down beside me!

His wet fur pressed against me;
Each of us warmed the other;
Each of us felt, in the stormy dark,
That beast and man were brother.

And when the falling forest
No longer crashed in warning,
Each of us went from our hiding place
Forth in the wild, wet morning.

How do clouds stay up in the sky?

Question asked by Joseph Coleman, aged $8\frac{1}{2}$

From *100½ Questions. Ask Uncle Albert* by Russell Stannard

Clouds are made of droplets of water. Water is heavier than air. So you're quite right: the clouds ought to drop out of the sky! And yet they don't.

I have a confession to make, Joseph. When I got your letter, I was shocked. I didn't know the answer. A *professor of physics* and I hadn't a clue why the clouds stayed up there! I felt very silly.

But it wasn't long before I began to feel a bit better. You see, I walked down the corridor at the university where I work, and I asked nearly all the other physicists your question. (I pretended I knew the answer, and was just testing them.) And do you know what? Not one of them had a clue either! Oh, they came up with all sorts of ideas as to what *might* be going on, but it turned out none of them was right. Not only did none of us have the answer, it had never occurred to any of us even to ask the question. That's often how it is in science. There can be some problem sitting right under everyone's nose (or in this case, sitting above their heads), and no on even notices that it is a problem. Then along comes some genius – like my hero Einstein – who becomes the first person to ask, 'Hey, what's going on here?' And then comes some big scientific discovery. Usually these really big discoveries are made by quite young scientists – those whose thinking is still lively and flexible, unlike we older scientists whose thinking tends to get stuck in a groove.

That's why *you* came up with your question, and we didn't. (But don't get too excited; *someone* has already come up with your question, so you will have to think up another one in order to get your Nobel Prize.)

Now, just in case you're thinking I'm waffling on like this because I still don't know the answer, let me say I have now read a book on cloud physics and I now think I know what's happening.

Hot air rises carrying water molecules with it. The air cools and the droplets form to make a cloud. Because droplets are heavier than air, they start to fall through the air – which is what we expect to happen. But (and this is the important bit) the air they fall through is itself *still rising*. So in fact the droplets tend to be carried *upwards* with the upflowing air (though they don't go up quite as fast as the air, because they are falling through the air).

Right. Now you're thinking, 'OK, that explains why the cloud doesn't fall. But if the droplets are going up, why don't we see the cloud going *up*?'

The reason is that as fast as the droplets are swept upwards, more air and water molecules rise to fill the space they have left. It is now the turn of these water molecules to cool down and form water droplets in the same place as the first lot – before they themselves are swept upwards too. So, that way the bottom of the cloud stays where it is and seems not to be moving. But actually the cloud is continually *replacing itself*. As fast as old cloud moves upwards, new cloud takes its place.

It's a bit like what happens on the motorway. An AA man looks at the TV monitors and reports severe congestion between Junctions 6 and 8. An hour later he reports that the situation has not changed. As far as he is concerned, the TV monitors are showing exactly the *same* sort of picture. But that doesn't, of course, mean that he is looking at the same set of cars. The traffic is slowly moving; the cars he saw earlier have been replaced by another lot, but the shape and density of the traffic looks much the same. ■

Fairy Rings

There's a great deal of folklore and superstition about mushrooms and toadstools. Perhaps this is because fungi seem to appear from nowhere, and mysteriously disappear again. And some, of course, are poisonous. The names of some fungi tell us that they were associated with supernatural beings: *Witches' Butter, Orange Elf-Cup, Fairies' Bonnets.*

The fruit bodies of some fungi grow in circles, and where this happens there is often a ring of short or dead grass inside a ring of longer, darker grass. People used to think that these circles were caused by fairies dancing in a circle at night; so they became known as 'fairy rings'. Another popular belief was that they were caused by lightning.

The scientific explanation is shown in Fig. 1. The fungus has a 'root system' (the *mycelium*) of tiny fibres which grows in an expanding circle. The fruit bodies of the fungus grow around the circumference of the mycelium, rather like flowers grow near the ends of the branches of a tree.

Fig. 1 *Fruit bodies growing around the edge of the mycelium.*

Fig. 2 explains those different rings of grass. The ring of short or dead grass is where the growing fungus has taken the nutrients from the soil. The ripe fruit body puts nutrients *back into* the soil, so the grass just outside the mycelium grows taller and greener.

taller, greener grass

fruit bodies

ordinary grass

short or dead grass

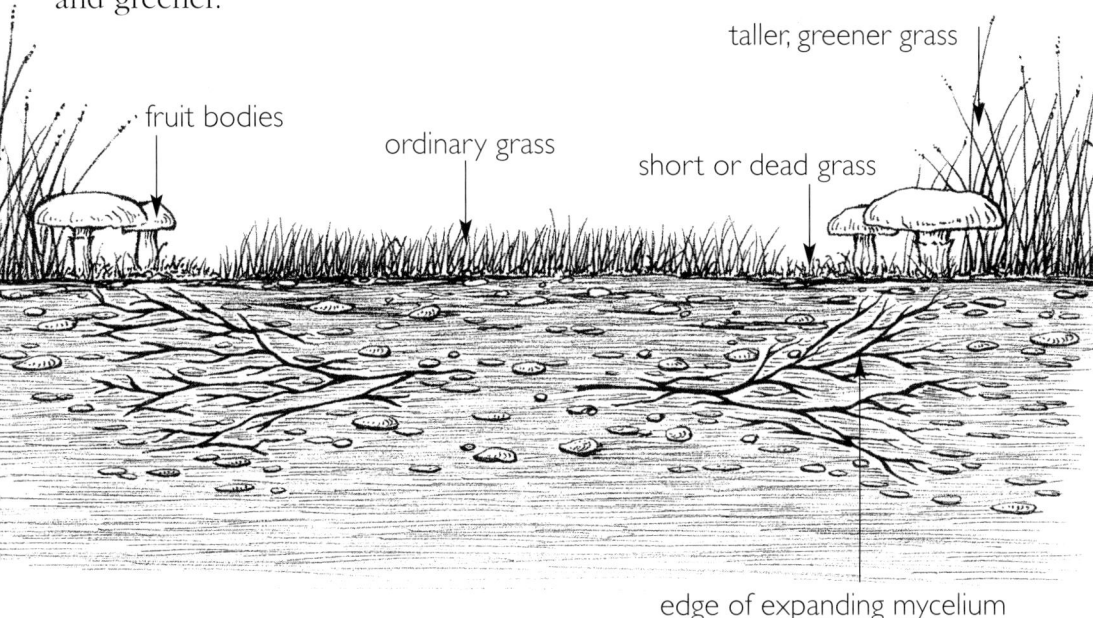

edge of expanding mycelium

Fig. 2 *Cross-section of a fairy ring*

People used to think that fungi were ephemeral, that they had very short lives. Now that we understand that the mycelium and its fruit bodies are a single fungus, we know this is not true. In America there is a single Honey Fungus which covers an area of 15 hectares – that's nearly the size of two soccer pitches. Naturalists estimate that it is around 1500 years old. So although the fruit bodies of a fungus are indeed ephemeral, its underlying mycelium may well be one of the oldest living things on the planet.

There is more about mushrooms on pages 16 and 46.

Marbles

William Bavin

MODERN MACHINE-MADE MARBLES

Sizes from 12.5mm–35mm ($\frac{1}{2}$in–1$\frac{1}{2}$in). Condition categories same as antiques. There are thousands of different names given to each type of machine-made marble so we are only going to describe the general categories.

Clears
Almost every colour you can imagine is now available as a clear glass marble.

Inserts, Leaf
The most popularly produced marble for fifty years from the 1920s to the 1970s. An individual pot of coloured glass is used to inject a leaf of colour into a mass of clear glass. The leaf can have several canes and can be of a single colour or of mixed colours.

Inserts, Spaghetti, Cat Eyes
Same process as described with leaf, but the effect is a random scattering of twisted canes within the glass.

Glass Chinas
Opaque glass with stripes of colour on the surface. A huge variety of different coloured stripes have been used over the years on different backgrounds. This type were amongst the earliest machine marbles produced. Manufacturers often tried to reproduce the look of natural agate.

Opaques
A completely plain opaque colour, now produced like the clears in a large number of colours.

Spotted (opaque or clear)
Chips of coloured glass are rolled into the surface of the marble before it is cooled.

Frosted (opaque or clear)
A finished marble is treated in an acid bath. The process can make an uninteresting marble great.

Lustered (opaque or clear)
The application of chemicals by spray to the skin of a marble as it is being made produces this irridescent effect. They are known as rainbows, oilies, pearls, or lustres.

Style and Feature Links

Formal/official language
The Field Mushroom 46
A Guide to the U.N. Convention .. 74
Convention on the Rights of
   the Child.. 75
Fairy Rings................................... 108
Marbles 110

Humorous verse
Limericks 63
An Attempt at Unrhymed Verse... 68
My Last Nature Walk 69
It's Spring, It's Spring 90
House Flies 93
The Fly 93
U.S. Flies in Hamburgers 94

Implicit/multi-layered meanings in poems
Mushrooms 16
Calligram.. 66
'You're Right,' said Grandad......... 70
Caterpillar 86
A Fly.. 91
The Fly 92

Narrative structure: passage of time
Janet's Last Book 28
The Tripods 54
The Snow-Walker's Son................. 58

TV/film comparisons
Gulliver's Travels 6
The Borrowers 8
Peter Pan.. 22
The Tempest................................... 25
Birds, Beasts and Relatives............ 33
The Wolves of Willoughby
   Chase... 51

Viewpoints in novels
Gulliver's Travels 6
The Borrowers 8
The Snow-Walker's Son................. 58
The December Rose....................... 61
Goggle Eyes 82
White Fang 98
White Wolf 100